A Compulsive Gardener: The Story of Burrow Farm Gardens

MARY BENGER

RIGHT Archway and
door leading down to
Millennium Garden with
the view to the hills and
valley beyond

A Compulsive Gardener: The Story of Burrow Farm Gardens

First published in the United Kingdom in 2019.

© Mary Benger 2019

ISBN 978-1-5272-4492-4

Printed and bound in the United Kingdom by Short Run Press.

This book is dedicated to my father Philip Newcomb who opened my eyes to the beauty and wonder of nature.

I would like to thank Kaye Hadfield for putting down on paper the various thoughts and ideas I have had during my making of this garden and trying to 'pin me down' to ordering these reminiscences in a logical way.

Russell Goffe-Wood for layout and design. Barbara Spender for her general tidying up of the text. Jo Whitworth, Sue Deere, Sally Newcomb, Nicola Stocken and Mark Bolton for some of their empathetic photographs.

IMAGE Watercolour by my daughter Penny Pritchard: Bluebells in profusion under oak trees in Burrow Farm Gardens

Foreword

How do you create a garden in such beautiful scenery? The rolling green hills and hedge-bounded fields of the Devon/Somerset border country are so enthralling that it is difficult to imagine creating something that could hope to compete. That Mary Benger has done so is testament to courage and determination as well as imagination.

I have always enjoyed my visits to Burrow Farm, too infrequent though they have been. It is a very beautiful place; and it is a place to see a wide and interesting range of plants, well-grown, well-situated, well-combined. Even more, it is somewhere to see a confident and relaxed planting style: plants running into each other, self-seeding, spreading, mingling. The scale of the garden always amazes me, it is big enough to show off some wonderful tree/shrub/lawn planting combinations, and big enough to play its part in the landscape and not be overpowered by it. I also, perhaps rather cheekily, imagine a series of battles over the years between Mary and John, her farmer husband, as she nibbled away more and more of his farm, turning productive pasture into border, lawn and shrubbery. It is nice to see that this process of change in the landscape is acknowledged here in the book in a gently humorous way and, one assumes, the success of Burrow Farm Gardens as a family business has led to her triumphant vindication. Farming is a difficult business at the best of times, something that the supermarket customer clutching a carton of organic artisan yogurt with a cartoon picture of a smiling cow on the side has almost no idea of. Mary's 'diversification' of the farm has clearly turned out to be a smart business move, and indeed it is interesting to read here of how Mary always had this idea of the garden as a business. How very forward looking!

I am amongst the many who love gardens that are relaxed in their approach to management and design. The maintenance here keeps everything looking under control but lets go in just the right places. There is plenty of self-seeding, and in certain areas, borders segue into meadow or other wilder, less managed vegetation. Such 'gardening with a light touch' can be a lot more difficult than traditional maintenance, and when employing people, there is the challenge of conveying it to staff too. That this seems to happen here to a remarkably successful degree is a testament to good management and teamwork.

One of the big changes in gardening since Mary started making the garden in 1963 has been the growth in garden design. Of course, I work in garden design, I make money writing about it, I lecture about it, some of my best friends are garden designers, but oh how I sometimes wish that this discipline had never taken off in the way it has done! A putative Mary today, eyeing their newly acquired acres, would probably employ a designer, and the garden would for ever more

LEFT Summerhouse with *Ammi visnaga* and *Echium vulgare* 'Blue Bedder', both annuals, and purple penstemon: Sally Newcomb

ABOVE The scarlet *Tulipa sprengeri* showing up well against the variegated iris growing in the pond below

RIGHT View through the woodland walk framed by a rhododendron in full bloom

be the designer's, with the same character and stamp of all their other gardens. The making of gardens the traditional way, by owners feeling, planting and cutting their way through a process of trial and error to create something unique, is now so much rarer. Which is a shame, as I believe that it has limited many people's creativity. The traditional process of gradual horticultural self-education has given the British Isles its unique richness and diversity of garden heritage. Burrow Farm is a garden that has clearly evolved organically, gradually and gently flowing and flowering over the curves of its landscape. It feels a lot more individual because of this, and its form and layout help make it possible to appreciate its story and evolution.

Here, Mary tells this story and explains the garden's evolution. And she does so in a way that is very articulate, something that not every creative garden maker is capable of doing. I was fascinated for example, by her discussion of her reaction to the 'rooms' concept, that classic element of English Arts and Crafts garden design, her feelings about how it might work in this landscape or might not, and her eventual compromise. The book has plenty of these 'thinkings-aloud', which actually makes it a potentially useful book too for other garden makers who want to resist the blandishments of the garden design professional and do it for themselves. I certainly hope it encourages more people to do so.

NOEL KINGSBURY

ABOVE Evergreen azaleas in the foreground across a serpentine wall with *Betula utilis* var. *jacquemontii* in the background

Contents

Introduction

A Brief Overview:
Planting, People and Personalities

Planting

Burrow Farm Gardens is a thirteen-acre garden of sweeping lawns, mature trees, and shrubs lying in a Devon valley, situated between Honiton and Axminster. The naturalistic planting has been designed to reflect the changing and often fickle moods of nature. It is a garden for all seasons, from the abundant snowdrops and hellebores that herald the spring to the vibrancy of the perennial borders in the summer.

With the approach of autumn the gardens are transformed by a seasonal display of brilliant and vibrant yellows, fiery reds and oranges as the trees and shrubs prepare for the long dark months ahead. And as winter bites, the haunting skeletal silhouettes of the many mature trees dominate, taking centre stage against the backdrop of a constantly changing Devon sky.

The old gnarled field maple now situated in the Woodland Garden was the original inspiration for starting the garden in earnest in 1963. Long ago this part of the garden was a Roman clay quarry that, over the centuries, was colonised by a mass of wildflowers situated amongst a variety of mature

rhododendrons. The garden gradually evolved from here, beginning with the creation of paths and walkways and a focus on the planting of a variety of trees, shrubs and herbaceous perennials.

The Rose Garden was the next area of significant development. It began to take shape in 1985 and was designed to make the maximum use of a narrow stretch of land between the edge of the garden and a neighbouring farm. The focal point of this garden is a stone statue, 'The Shy Maiden', standing in the centre of a froth of *Nepeta racemosa* 'Walker's Low'.

Another well-established part of Burrow Farm Gardens is the Terrace Garden, its formal layout filled with 'cottage style' planting structured by stonework, a small summerhouse, gravel paths, steps and fastigiate pear trees, *Pyrus calleryana* 'Chanticleer'. In 2000, to celebrate the Millennium, the next enterprise in what were now maturing

gardens began to take shape – a formal, colour themed garden with a central rill leading to a pond that is well-stocked with plants and fish. A traditional stone gazebo was designed as a vantage point from which to make the most of the stunning rural views over the valley towards Axminster and beyond. Seven years later, in 2007, an area covered with brambles was cleared and became what is now known as Azalea Glade. Amongst the azaleas and rhododendrons grow a variety of ferns, primulas and choice bulbs enjoying their position in the dappled shade provided by mature trees such as magnolias, acers and cornus. Last but not least, to celebrate the garden's fiftieth anniversary, the Grasses or Anniversary Garden was created in 2013. Ornamental grasses were planted above a sunken path and these grasses now wave gently over a profusion of perennials with a pink, blue and purple palette.

People

A great many people have been involved in the creation of the garden over the years. They range from the Benger family themselves to the gardeners, the volunteers like John and Peggy Perryman who were the first, and of course Fred Peadon, and more recently students from various horticultural courses based in France who come to help out and gain horticultural experience in a different context. Just a few of the people who have played major parts are mentioned here and their introduction is partly necessary because of the confusing number of 'Johns' who have appeared over the years and are referred to in this book.

A special mention must be given here to Michael, our grandson. Michael is my mainstay. As well as being keen on the gardens, he is the website organiser, advertiser and in general sees to all the clerical jobs I hate doing, to say nothing of being the stone wall builder now that John Hawkins is no longer with us.

Family

John Benger: My long-suffering husband who has had to put up with my gardening obsession.

Tony Benger: Our son, who has a large landscaping business.

Penny: Our daughter, who is a talented garden designer.

Jane: Our daughter, the only one of my immediate family not involved in gardening but she 'does' the bookkeeping.

Sue-Sue: Our youngest daughter, who runs the tearoom in the garden.

Grandchildren: We have ten grandchildren and three of them are involved in different capacities in Tony's landscaping business or in Burrow Farm Gardens.

Extended 'family'

John Hawkins: My part-time helper in the garden for thirty-eight years and the person responsible for building and maintaining most of the garden's stonework.

John and Judy Gill: The two people who provided major encouragement in the early years.

Judy, Lynne, Karen, Madeline, Jacky, Kaye and Annie: My lady 'weeders' (and much more).

Edward and Shaun: they do most of the mowing and many other 'heavy' jobs'.

Personalities

LEFT Mary and Michael planting an acer in Azalea Glade: Nicola Stocken

BELOW Daisy the collie posing among the bluebells

FOLLOWING PAGES *Diascia personata* contrasting the purple berberis backed by silver *Elaeagnus angustifolia* 'Quicksilver'. Hypericum with colourful berries and penstemon can be seen in the foreground: Sally Newcomb

Burrow Farm Gardens would not be the same place without its four-legged friends. They are part of its ambience and warmth. Some are mentioned in the book so need a short introduction at this point. Fly, Peter and Tilly, my faithful border collies over many years, were all rescues from various places; Davis and Smith, both collie crosses; Jill, a stray greyhound; and Sheba, Lucy and Willow, all German Shepherds.

The book describes more fully how Burrow Farm Gardens was created and developed. If you have visited the gardens it is written so that you can 'dip in' and find out about a favourite part of the garden in more detail and depth, how it started and how it has changed over time. If you have not visited

before it is written to 'whet your appetite' and encourage you to come and see us. This is a book about the creation of Burrow Farm Gardens as they are today, the people that have helped me along the way, the joys, the ups and downs reflected in the valley it looks over, and the lessons learnt. These are woven throughout the narrative. They are a reflection of my learning about perspective, structure, plants, planting and plant combinations, all designed to produce the naturalistic effect that was my vision when I began work on the gardens more than fifty years ago.

Although each chapter deals with an area of the garden and can be read more like a series of stand-alone pieces, the connecting thread running through all of them is my particular experience of naturalistic gardening, aimed at doing justice to the land we have and the valley the gardens sit in. That vista has guided me in planning and developing the gardens as I sit looking at it in its various guises through all seasons and weathers and from a range of viewing platforms. With this landscape and its particular focal points I have learnt about perspective and balance. Whether you have acres or a small plot, I hope the book will go some way in helping you to make or re-create your own naturalistic space where our wild and native plants jostle with, and thrive alongside, the plethora of indigenous and newly introduced plants we all 'must have' and love to grow.

It goes without saying that this is not a book about gardening as such. There are already many gardening books out there, a fair few of which are in my possession. I do not intend this book to 'tread on these toes', neither am I sure how much I could add to this vast and erudite body of knowledge. The chapters that follow are written to provide a colourful and lively portrait of the garden, the family, the people who have worked here over the years and the various animals that are as much part of the gardens as the plants.

Chapter 1

From Farm to Gardens: In the Beginning

'Which one of you is the gardener then?' This was the first question our new neighbours asked. As newly-weds about to embark on establishing a dairy farm, we had of course asked ourselves many questions but, unsurprisingly, this was not one of them. In the silence that followed I reluctantly replied 'It looks as though I'll be doing the garden then'. That moment marked the beginning of the fifty plus years, and still counting, that I've spent creating Burrow Farm Gardens.

Initially, our priority was to build a dairy herd of Friesians and get the house as comfortable as we could. John was fully occupied for most of that time, and many years to come, in buying and looking after our herd of Friesian cows. When I eventually got the time, my gardening endeavours inevitably started around the house. As my obsession with gardening grew the boundary fence surreptitiously edged outwards yard by yard. And as I appropriated more and more land I realised that I had been the willing pupil of an excellent teacher. My father had been a very keen gardener. As a child you do not realise how much you are actually picking up in the way of knowledge. I must have subconsciously stored up names and good locations for the range of plants he grew as I followed him around our family garden in Kent and I did not appreciate this until I started my own garden in Devon.

I think, initially, my father encouraged me

by giving me a very prominent bit of garden when I was a small child. It was definitely not a tucked away plot where nothing would grow and no one could see it. We selected annuals and I sowed the seeds and looked after them as they grew from seedlings to mature plants. An elderly aunt used to give me six pansies for my birthday. She would take me into town where I always spent ages choosing which colours I wanted for that year. I loved planting and watering and realised very early on the value of dead-heading in prolonging the flowering season.

Unfortunately, my father died when I was seventeen so he never saw Burrow Farm Gardens but I think he would have loved it. The strange thing is that when a cousin of mine, who was quite a bit older than me, visited and walked around he told me that it was just the sort of garden my father would have planted, with that mix of formality and informality that he would have aimed for and which also harmonises and blends with the garden's natural situation on the side of a Devon valley.

When we first moved to Burrow Farm in 1959 there was nothing that could claim to be a garden, just an asbestos bungalow and corrugated iron sheds with the potential to become a working dairy farm and its setting overlooking a captivating Devon valley. Oddly enough, although the view has become such an integral part of the garden, I had not seen it until the day after we actually moved here. John, my new husband, had been to see the property on his own and thought it had potential as a dairy farm. When we both came down later, it was in the thickest fog you can possibly imagine. I can remember saying to him 'What's the view like?' His answer was on the lines of 'Well it's a valley, it's this and it's that and oh, by the way, it's got a nice view'.

When we eventually moved in we came with a caravan because the house was uninhabitable. It had taken so long for our very ancient Land Rover to tow the caravan from Surrey to Devon that we arrived after dark. Neither of us could remember what was here and what was not, so we stopped half way down the drive and stayed there for the night. The next morning I opened the curtains and the rolling green hills, dappled with their own particular light, so typical of this part of Devon, were revealed in all their glory. It was a complete and wonderful surprise but we had no time to waste staring at such breath-taking beauty because our immediate surroundings could not have been more of a contrast, dominated as they were by large sheets of old corrugated iron and dilapidated chicken houses. Everything was an absolute tip and, of course, we had to prioritise the farm and dairy herd but the thought of that view stayed with me through all the highs and lows of establishing our home and farm.

The first priority was the house. We sorted and cleaned just one room so we could put a bed in it. We had no electricity and no mains water. There were mains services down at the farm but not in the house. The garden to the house had one laburnum tree and about fifty Brussels sprout plants, and that was it, but gardening had to take a back seat as we struggled with the house and setting up and establishing the farm. I clearly remember feeling thirsty one night, making my way outside to the water butt, turning on the tap and filling a glass. I drank half and went back

to bed. In the morning I looked at a half glass of water seething with little tiny worms. If ever I wanted to be sick, it was then, but luckily I had no ill effects.

Before the builders put in the plumbing we had no bathroom, just a little hut outside that served as our toilet. It was really basic, a hole in the ground with a seat and the added flourish of a little mouse hole at seat level. So the first thing I did was to stuff a cabbage stalk in the hole but by the next day it had been nibbled completely away. That kept me on the edge of the seat for months and it marked the start of my battle with the mouse inhabitants of Burrow Farm, one that has carried on to this day. Over the years they have gorged themselves regularly on my plants and established many desirable little residences in the choicest locations in the garden.

Burrow Farm Gardens, as it is now, is as much about my family and the dogs that have grown up and lived in them as the gardens themselves. Over our years of married life John and I have had four children, Tony, Penny, Jane and Sue-Sue, who all now live locally and have families of their own. Changes have inevitably happened. We built a new house to replace the original old asbestos bungalow and the Farm has gradually been transformed and absorbed into the gardens which many of the family now work in, or are associated with, while the Friesian herd has been replaced by other four legged friends, especially horses and dogs. It would be fair to say that the dogs in particular have become central to the life of the gardens. Everyone working here knows of my approach when they see Tilly, my current Border Collie rescue dog and my constant shadow.

Dogs have always been a part of my life from a very early age. As a child we had Cairn Terriers and I can vividly remember our coalman's German Shepherd, which could shake hands. To me this was the most wonderful thing ever but try teaching a Cairn

BELOW Sheba, who was the first of my many rescue dogs. She was the reason for the beginning of my career in dog training

to shake hands – no way, no. I never gave up on the idea but I had to wait until my teens before I could make my dreams into a reality. One day, cycling to school, I passed a house with a young puppy tied up to a kennel. I asked the daughter of the house about it and was told her family could not keep it. Her brother had come across it on army exercises out on the common in Surrey. A small puppy on its own could not be left, so her brother volunteered to take it back with him but now they needed to find it a permanent home. I looked at it and thought it looked like a young German Shepherd. I desperately wanted to take it home but my parents were adamant they did not want it. But I was equally determined to have it so I hatched a plan. I had quite a big basket on the front of my bike and one Friday morning

I cycled to school as usual, stopped at the house, knocked on the door and said I would give the puppy a home. I arrived home that Friday evening with the dog in the basket. My parents were furious. I told them they would be murderers if they did not let me keep it and all sorts of things like that. In the end I wore them down until they relented slightly and said I could keep it for the weekend but had to take it back the following Monday. I put it in the calf pens and looked after it all weekend while I worked on them. The puppy was so good they extended their ultimatum to a week and that was the beginning of my first rescue. But for years afterwards my mother reminded me of my uncharacteristic bad behaviour.

While still growing, and to sort of pay me back I suppose, the puppy kept going to

our neighbours and killing their chickens.
I soon got fed up with using all my pocket
money on replacements. I asked for, and
tried out, all the different advice I was given,
including tying the dead chicken round her
neck, but with no success. That last remedy
was gruesome and of course she hated it, so
in the end, in desperation, I decided she had
to be trained. I heard of some dog training
classes in Surrey and we started to go to them.
She responded quite well and, out of the blue,
as things seem to happen in life, I became
interested in training dogs.

Initially when I left school, I had a brief
spell working in a Department Store in
Guildford. I had met John by then and we
decided that, as you got a staff discount,
I should try for the china department at
Harveys rather than fashion or anything
like that because we were saving up to get
married and had no china. At the interview
I must have overplayed my interest in china
and found myself being whisked off to
Staffordshire for training to become the Royal
Doulton representative for Guildford. I did

the job for about a year but it was difficult
because John had the weekends off while I
had to work on Saturdays. I had Wednesdays
free, but of course he was working and so
was everyone else I knew. Over that time
too, various things happened in the family.
My father died and my mother wanted to
move somewhere else so, with no real regrets,
I handed in my notice. The people who ran
the dog training in Guildford suggested that
until I moved and married, I should help run
their dog training kennels. I went along and
after the first week they asked me to become
a full-time trainer. I did various dog-training
competitions with my now fully-grown and
trained dog that was definitely a German
Shepherd and also, I suppose inevitably,
became the owner of a collie puppy. This was
the beginning of a lifelong interest in collies.

You may think this is an irrelevant
diversion in an account about the creation
of Burrow Farm Gardens, but my love of
dogs has been passed onto my children.
Dogs are very much part of the fabric of life
in the gardens. From the waifs and strays

that have turned up here to those that have been knowingly rescued, the dogs have managed to weave their stories into most of the accounts of the development of different parts of Burrow Farm Gardens and almost every chapter of the book. The gardens simply would not be the same without them.

As I grew older, other gardens were also a big influence on me. Visiting Sissinghurst and Hidcote, I discovered that I very much liked the idea of garden 'rooms' but, for me, their drawback was that these 'rooms' were constructed with hedges and walls. I could

not see myself developing something like that in the same way because we are on a hillside and every 'room' constructed would be looking onto the rolling hills and valleys so characteristic of East Devon. Sissinghurst's kind of formality did not, to my mind, 'fit' our location. I can clearly remember sitting in one garden I visited and trying to analyse why something seemed to be a complete and very appealing picture one way but if you looked the other way it didn't have the same sense of harmony and satisfaction. I spent a long time trying to work out why this should be. I realised that it was all about balance and if it was possible to provide a mix of a few evergreens and other types of trees, shrubs and perennials with different and contrasting shapes on either side of your viewpoint, you could provide that balance. I decided to try and create the same feeling of rooms myself at Burrow Farm but to do it predominately using shrubs and trees as my formal structure and as a way of providing tantalising glimpses to the natural vista beyond. By planting these 'rooms' in flowing and billowing lines I thought I could echo the natural geography of the countryside beyond the gardens. Quite simply that is the way the garden has developed over the years, a series of sketches and pictures with the surrounding natural geography providing the informal frames. Again, when I think about it, I am not sure if this is the influence of my father because he was a keen photographer as well as gardener. It is more than possible that my thoughts of creating the garden as a series of pictures came from his influence.

The little bit of garden I worked on round the farmhouse soon became insufficient for my ambitions so I gradually began to move outwards. John told me I had to stop taking little bits of land or the cows would be short of grass. In exasperation at my surreptitious 'land grab' he offered me the old clay pit some way from the house in a bid to curb my growing plant obsession and keep vital grass for the herd. I had just been to visit Knightshayes Court and as a result realised that a garden in a wood was feasible, and it was something I had not considered before. The kernel of Burrow Farm Gardens was laid down from that point, although I did not know it at the time.

I remember the first two plants I ever bought and when I bought them in my very first year at Burrow Farm in the winter of 1960 and they show exactly how little I knew about gardening. There used to be an auction in Honiton and I bought two trees. I knew exactly what I wanted to do with them. In my mind the important thing was to place these two trees at the right distance apart to swing a hammock. I planted the trees in perfect alignment and the appropriate distance apart but to this day and fifty or so years later, I've never bought the hammock, let alone had the time to sit and relax. The two trees were a *Robinia pseudocacia* and a *Malus* 'Wisley Crab'. Thinking back I probably bought them because they looked as though they had strong trunks. That was my only condition for the purchase – as long as I could swing a hammock between them it was fine. At

the time they were right in the corner of the garden but now they both stand proudly outside the conservatory and tearoom, so a hammock is out of the question. And of course I've now, regretfully, come to terms with the fact that my hammock swinging days are over.

Over the years the garden has attracted a range of characters (not counting children and conscripts of course), drawn to its ethereal beauty, framed at different times by the mists rolling in off the sea, the rain sweeping over the valley in great grey curtaining sweeps, the sun lighting up its contours, and the glowering clouds setting off its verdant greens.

John and Peggy Perryman were my very first garden volunteers. They used to come one afternoon a week and worked so hard. John used to do my garden accounts. In fact he was a high-powered businessman and got huge pleasure out of my basic money organising – which was if there was no money in the ice cream pot then no money could be spent. I have still got the ice cream pot!

Another significant 'conscript' to the garden was Fred. He was long past retirement

BELOW Fred Peadon in his eighties with his trusty Haytorette mower that he used like a zimmer frame

age but invaluable to me in the sense that, unlike any other members of the family, he never seemed to think any of my projects was impossible. He would listen in silence to me explaining some of my more ambitious ideas, then there would be a brief pause and he would say 'What tools shall us use, Mary?' Fred had never really had any dealings with things mechanical so when I tried to teach him how to use the Haytorette mower I was initially met with what can only be described as a great deal of resistance. Eventually he mastered it and was never happier than when he was shuffling around the lawn using the mower as a prototype Zimmer frame. When the garden expanded sufficiently to justify a 'ride on' mower Fred was fiercely protective of his Haytorette. In his eyes the 'ride on' would never rival and should not replace his precious machine. I think he was afraid of being made redundant along with the mower. Just a few weeks after Fred died the 'ride on' broke down and I had to take it to Crewkerne in the horse box to be mended. As I passed the cemetery

where Fred was buried I was sure I could hear him muttering 'I told you that mower was no good'.

Over my gardening career I have done quite a few commercial gardens. My daughter Penny, who has now taken over from me, working for Tony in his garden landscaping business, says if she is going round the villages in a locality or re-doing any of the gardens years on, she always knows if it was 'one of mine'. She can see my character and influence through the plants that have been planted and by the way they have been used.

I think a garden reflects the person or people creating it. Of course others become involved along the way and there are those who follow who inevitably bring their own thoughts and influences. In this way, and with the ebb and flow of time, a garden changes through different kinds of beauty, reflecting everything from care and promise to neglect and decay, while its atmosphere and presence throughout these cycles remain undaunted.

Chapter 2

From Ancient Roman Clay Pit to a Secret Garden: The Woodland Garden

LEFT Woodland Garden with *Rhododendron* 'Orange Beauty' and *Acer campestre* seen framing the steps winding through the trees

The garden around the house was gradually expanding. By this time I had turned the Brussels sprout area into a lawn, the Brussels had been relocated to a new vegetable patch and I was acquiring more plants. Also, as the children grew I had more time to myself. We had quite a few big rocks around the farm in various places in the fields that John wanted to get rid of, so he used to bring them in the transport box and tip them over at the side of the drive to the house and I started to create a rock garden, particularly as alpines were a range of plants that caught my eye and gave me a great deal of pleasure.

Around this time, and as luck would have it, my visit to 'Treasures' at Tenbury Wells left me with the overwhelming feeling that a perfect day out was a visit to a garden followed by a blissful browse round the adjoining 'plant sales' area and a tasty homemade tea. My garden visits began in earnest. A similar day spent at Knightshayes Court impressed on me the attractions of creating a garden in a wood, so when John began to rebel at my eyeing up more field to extend the garden, I suggested that it might perhaps be a good idea if I turned my attentions to the huge Roman clay pit that was in one of our fields. I knew that my interest in alpines would not help me in the development of a two-acre garden in a wood of huge oak trees so I would need to extend my gardening repertoire. Although I kept doing the garden round the house, my secret

walk was to the clay pit. I developed a split gardening personality – one where I gardened in full view with Alpines and the other where I sketched out my designs mentally and gardened in secret. When John told me I 'could do what I liked down there' he could not have envisaged that I would be there clearing, digging, planting and weeding for the next fifty years.

The only drawback was that the area was some distance from the house. My joy at making my way down what became my secret path to 'the quarry', or clay pit, sustained me through what proved to be the sheer hard work necessary to create my 'garden in a wood'. I think from the very beginning I felt that this secret place could be special. Dominating everything was a marvellous and ancient field maple, *Acer campestre*, with a gnarled trunk of some girth growing amongst a sea of brambles. Around the bole of that tree, violets, bluebells and primroses grew in profusion, creating an oasis of natural beauty. There were other little spots dotted throughout the area that were also naturally wonderful.

That tree was really the start of it all. It became the guide that shaped my garden philosophy. Along the way I have tried to garden naturally alongside those wild flowers where appropriate. We garden here now with that specific thought of maintaining this balance in mind. The campions have to be pulled out in some places and not in others,

ABOVE *Allium triquertum*
and bluebells in the
bog garden with
Primula pulverulenta
and the large leaved
Lysichiton americanus,
skunk cabbage, in
the background. A
rhododendron of the
grande series can be seen
on the right

violets allowed in some places and not others.
This is where I really began learning about the
sort of gardener I was.

The area itself looked over the valley
towards one particular hill with a domed top.
Usually, hills have a hedgerow or something
going along them, but not this hill. Hills
like this are remnants of ancient activity and
pepper the landscape throughout this part of
Devon. There is a well-known Roman clay
pit in the vicinity of Burrow Farm and my
'hole in the ground' or Woodland Garden, as
we call it now, is very similar to that clay pit
but actually much, much bigger. John used
to delight in teasing me when I first started
down there by saying that if the council got
to hear of the pit they would requisition it as
a dump or designate it as a site of historical
interest and that would be the end of my
garden. In that sense it was my very own
secret garden.

One of the earliest things to happen as I
started thinking about making a woodland
garden was the fire that swept through our
caravan. It happened in the night. We did not
report it ourselves because we knew nothing
about it but people across the valley saw the
flames and called the fire engine. By the time
we realised what had happened it was well
alight. We told the fire crew that it was past
saving and they might just as well let it burn,
but as they had been alerted to the incident
they had no choice but to put the fire out
and liberally douse it with water. Only the
shell of the caravan remained, leaving us with
the problem of what to do with it. We tried
to set fire to it again so we could get rid of
the rest at a later date but it would not burn
because everything that was flammable had
already gone. We decided that the only way to
dispose of this shell and chassis was to push it
down into the old clay pit where it joined all

the other rubbish we had been forced to get rid of over the years like the old corrugated iron buildings and a load of rusty tin. This spot had become our designated rubbish tip and I little thought that in the future I would want to create a garden down here. Initially as I started clearing my new plot I tried screening this unsightly area but that was unsuccessful so eventually we got a digger in to bury the eyesore and then sculpt it by putting topsoil on everything. For years the ground bounced slightly as you walked over it. The children loved it because they had a lawn that you could actually bounce on.

Because the area was located some distance from the house it was essential to build a rudimentary shelter to protect me from the rain that sweeps the area. Whether it's the fine misty drizzle that blows in eerily off the sea and is so characteristic around here or the

Devon deluge that can last for days, it still soaks you. Two sheets of corrugated iron and some salvaged wooden posts were big enough to shelter me, with the addition of a few tools.

In the beginning the site was an unfriendly mass of brambles, fallen trees and nettles that had become established over many years. I began by clearing this dense undergrowth using a wheelbarrow and a few hand tools. For years the farm drains had gone down through the area so it was extremely fertile, more so as you got down to the bottom. As the family grew, our four young children became co-conspirators in my endeavours. After all, what was there not to like about the endless succession of bonfires and your own bog that had to have channels dug through it to draw all the excess water flowing down the hill into the pond. That is the kind of gardening small children like.

RIGHT Richard Lawrence with the digger burying the old caravan, tin and corrugated iron that we had dumped in the quarry over the years

ABOVE Our four children
helping me in the quarry
while German Shepherd,
Lucy, looks on as usual

I started by thinking woodland garden meant rhododendrons but it was all clay and I did not know whether they would 'do' or not. My solution to this problem was to go and dig up some wild *Rhododendron ponticum* from somewhere else and plant these out in various places to see what would happen. They sort of grew satisfactorily but the area was very shady and the plants were getting 'too drawn'. Luckily I had a friend, John Gill, who came to cast his eye over the plot. Between us we decided which trees would be better taken out and which I definitely wanted to keep. Then we marked them out. He knew the value of the timber and we worked out that we would also need to get rid of some 'good ones' to pay for the machinery we had to use to winch out the felled trees from the top. This was necessary as the site at this point was virtually inaccessible and the slopes so steep. They then had to be hauled away. It was important that the cost of the labour be covered by the value of the timber from these felled trees as I had no money in the 'gardening pot'. It

was finely judged. His calculations proved to be very accurate and I ended up with fifteen pounds. That fifteen pounds became my total budget for the garden. Then, it seemed to be a princely sum, now it seems like nothing, but to me it was the start of something special that would transform the two acres or so we were tackling.

In the beginning I worked the area entirely on my own. John was busy with the farm and thought the whole thing was a terrible idea anyway. Over the years the build-up of brambles, nettles and fallen trees had gradually obscured the whole area. It is not until you work a piece of land that paths become obvious because they appear where individuals naturally walk. To clear the ground I had to use chemicals with a knapsack sprayer. Climbing over the slopes with this contraption was not easy but it was the only way to tackle it. I could not get any real access until I had cleared a swathe with the trusty sprayer.

At this stage I did not sketch anything out

RIGHT Lucy and I with the knap-sack sprayer as I sprayed off the ever present brambles. I became adept at clambering over the steep slopes with this heavy piece of equipment on my back

ABOVE Making steps in the quarry with Tony. This is the kind of gardening that appeals to young boys. This was the beginning of Tony's step making which culminated years later with the grand flight of steps down the cliffs at Lyme Regis

RIGHT The view over the ha-ha with the lace cap *Hydrangea macrophylla* 'Blue Wave' in the foreground: Nicola Stocken

primulas from seed. These were my first plant love affair because they were right for the situation and performed well in natural drifts. From the start I was determined I was not going to spend a lot of time maintaining the area because it was hidden from view. Nobody knew what was happening down there so all I needed to do was keep it clear around each plant but I also felt I had to keep planting and planting because everything would take such a long time to mature.

The next stage was thinking about structures and that meant paths and steps. It was all very boggy down at the bottom and difficult to walk on, so a bit of a problem. Also, just as luck would have it, some friends of ours who lived in Pinhoe said that the nursery behind them was selling up and being demolished to make way for a building plot. John wanted to see if he could get some second hand water pipe so we went there for the viewing day. Amongst the various items for sale there were two huge great heaps of big slate slabs. Alongside these there was a little heap of about ten slabs that I thought would be ideal as paving for my paths, so I left a bid. I think it was probably about five pounds for the small heap of ten. That evening they rang me to tell me that for my five pounds I had got the two big heaps. I had calculated that if I had got the smaller heap I could get them in the back of our van and that would be fine. Two big heaps about twenty miles away meant that I had to hire a lorry. That was a big and unplanned expense but on the other hand I had these wonderful old slates. John used the tractor to get them to the top of the quarry and I manoeuvred them down the slopes. There is one particular one which I think is about five feet by three feet and every time I see it I think of the effort of getting it down there and the many trips to the osteopath that it caused.

More recently, our son Tony, who runs a landscaping business was asked to remove some grave edging from a local churchyard

because it was impossible. I had a vision and I had set my mind on it. To start with I just thought I would be making a lovely walk and garden for my own pleasure but I also had the feeling that I needed to make it financially viable, perhaps by opening the garden to the public. I reasoned that if I could not go on after the first ten years, the plants would at least have increased in value and I could sell them, so I was not wasting any money at that stage. The plants came from many sources. In exchange for taking John Gill's growing family of four a churn of six pints of milk in the car on the way to school, I was given shrubs and trees, including misshapen trees that he could not sell. All his plant 'waifs and strays' were welcome and gladly accepted by me and he let me use his trade account. I mainly bought rhododendrons and azaleas. I also grew

BELOW One of the many calves which I hand reared to finance the garden in the beginning

to allow for easy access for mowing. Most of them were lovely rough granite that he thought were too good to go in a skip. So home they came to be put in the PUMS heap (potentially useful materials) while the six foot ones made ideal risers for the steps we'd originally made using wood branches as risers to the grass treads. These had to be replaced every few years as they rotted and required a lot of maintenance.

As my plants grew I discovered the clay had been excavated in bays. Where there was a promontory it was difficult to get anything to grow because there were more stones in the clay, especially around the edges of the

bays, so it was all about what soil was where, because it varied hugely. Mostly it was just solid clay, very, very pure clay. We actually had a potter who came and took some of the clay to make some pots. He said it was the purest clay he had ever worked with, other than manufactured clay. I still have one of the pots he made.

Right down at the bottom of the area it was too wet for certain plants and right up at the top it was too dry for other plants to thrive. Somewhere in the middle, particularly where the leaf mould had built up from the ashes and oaks, was the most fertile soil and primulas did well at the bottom. Clay is very fertile. It is just that gardeners find it difficult to work with, although I admit you have got to find exactly the right time to do this.

I had no plan other than putting these pieces of the jigsaw together. I find that when you work an area you gradually get the feel of it, where certain plants need to be, where the natural access points are and the focal points or dots that draw the eye. The garden comes to you in this sense. And you have to have the patience to allow this to happen. When I started, this idea of naturalistic planting was ahead of its time really because the 60s were a lot more about formality, so I was a bit of a pioneer in that sense. For the garden at Burrow Farm the surroundings were so beautiful it was a matter of enhancing and working with the views over the valley rather than imposing myself on them.

I think at the time, the really difficult thing was scale. Taking a plant that was only about a foot high and planting it under one of those huge great oak trees meant the scale was so difficult to visualise. It was fine if you were planting ground cover like vinca but it was the plants that were eventually going to be fairly big but looked so insignificant for so many years that were more of an imponderable. I remember thinking that, probably, for the first ten years or so, you could walk around and hardly realise I had

ABOVE LEFT *Lysichiton camtschatcensis*, Asian skunk cabbage from Japan crossed with the American species to produce this cream coloured variety that has typical hybrid vigour growing in the bog garden

ABOVE RIGHT The yellow flowered *Lysichiton americanus*, known as the American skunk cabbage, flowering in March and April to be followed by enormous leaves giving a tropical feel to the Woodland Garden

done anything except a bit of clearance. At the start the brambles and nettles were taller than any of the plants I had put in but that did not worry me as long as I could see that they were all thriving and growing well.

To finance my growing gardening ambitions it was essential to generate an income to put back into the development of a growing garden. I was already augmenting my 'garden pot' by doing jobs like hand rearing calves on the farm and after a few years I felt ready to open the garden to the public. We started by opening for just the month of May, sold a few plants and served Devon cream teas on Sundays. This worked for several years

as it enabled me to spend the whole of the school holidays with my four children. They all had ponies, were keen on riding, and were enthusiastic members of the local pony club. It meant a very busy time for me taking them to horse shows, pony club rallies and pony club camp. At one time, and for several years, I organised the pony club camp at Burrow Farm for all the junior members. It was always 'touch and go' at these camps whether they enjoyed the riding or the swimming in our newly dug pool the most.

People always say to me how wonderful it must have been for our children to grow up with such a lovely garden but I can honestly

pond these will be fine for you'. Several times over the years I have been given plants by people who believe that because the garden is large it will be able to cope with the kind that are massively invasive. Actually I think it is people with small gardens who are better able to deal with these garden 'thugs' because they have more time to control them. I am still trying to eliminate those donated marginal plants from this part of the garden. I should have learnt my lesson from this time but I still accept unwanted plants because I cannot bear to see them consigned to the compost heap. Now this woodland garden has matured to the point where I am happy with areas of deep shade and moisture where the skunk cabbage, *Lysichiton americanus*, thrive, contrasted with dryer areas where wild flowers carpet the ground.

At the end of the first decade of gardening the clay pit there was a decision to be made. The plants were increasing in value and it was a question of whether to carry on, or dig them up and sell them. We decided to carry on. I knew from this point that it had to be a 'commercial' garden that had to pay for itself. With the clay pit it was just a matter of giving it a chance to grow but as a commercial enterprise the area had to be joined to the garden around the house. Originally there was just my narrow walk past the end of the house but this now had to be expanded in all directions. Forty years later I am still expanding the garden and the maintenance is getting more elaborate and detailed.

My two-acre garden in the wood is now part of the thirteen acres that make up the thriving commercial garden known as Burrow Farm Gardens. The gardens host thousands of visitors every year and I have had many compliments about them but one of the nicest I have ever had was from a little girl who said to me 'Mrs Benger, your garden just makes me feel I want to dance'. That is why I garden.

say they got more pleasure from making camps in the quarry with old corrugated iron sheets and cooking stinging nettles on a bonfire on the rubbish heap than they ever got from the garden. Such are children.

One very hot summer when the pond completely dried up, we seized the opportunity to deepen it. We hired a digger but soon discovered it was not as dry as we thought. The digger became bogged down and we had to hire a second one to dig the first one out – not a cheap exercise. I have had to be content with a shallow pond ever since and this has given me yet another problem. There is no depth in the middle to stop the more rampant marginal plants taking over the whole pond. Most of these have been donations from people who have handed them over saying 'you've got a big

Chapter 3

From Flowing Lawns to Focal Dots and Flourishes: Joining the Dots

LEFT I particularly like intermingling flowers of similar colour but different shapes. The dahlia here is 'Bishop's Children', which I raised from seed, and threading its way through the dark foliage of the dahlia is *Crocosmia aurea* 'Golden Ballerina'

At the beginning there were just very narrow walks down to the Woodland Garden. Now they've been expanded sideways, connecting the 'garden rooms' radiating out from the house. I certainly found developing the parts of the garden nearer the house a lot easier than negotiating the steep incline of the quarry. As I began to connect and join the different parts of the garden it was easier to work on those areas closest to the house because the ground was much flatter and Sue-Sue, my youngest, was a baby at the time. I could carry her backwards and forwards on my hip, a plant in the other hand and a spade over my shoulder. My mother also lived on the farm by then. Without her here to look after us and cook for us we would probably all have starved. Looking back on it I was lucky to be bitten by the gardening bug so young. I was nineteen when we came here and I know from experience you have a lot more energy then.

I always used to find that if I was encroaching out into any of the fields in 'bulges' John was less amenable than if I worked in straight lines. He hated me putting a 'bulge' in a fence but he did not mind me straightening it up. Quite rightly, I had to fight for every inch of my 'land grab'. More recently I have to confess, I did the huge planting of the azaleas in what is now dubbed Azalea Glade and John did not know about it for two years!! Rhododendrons and azaleas

have always been a great love of mine. Maybe it is because I was born in Kent where the soil is alkaline so they always seemed to be very special because we did not have them in our own garden. Then we moved to Surrey and used to visit Winkworth Arboretum regularly. I can remember to this day the steps going down through the deciduous azaleas to a lake at the bottom. To me, even as a young teenager, that was the most wondrous thing ever.

I think your influences as a child always come through in your gardens and although, by this time, I was gardening with a view to launching Burrow Farm Gardens as a commercial enterprise, I can honestly say that the gardens have never been, nor ever will be, a job. I garden for pleasure and the sheer joy of it. It has always been my garden and its development has had to be in the ways that appeal to me.

I have never felt the need to do something in the garden because it is judged to be highly fashionable. It is my garden first, and my very informal style. I am definitely not a slave to garden trends but have also always been inspired by the idea of making different 'garden rooms' because this approach seemed to suit the large spaces I was dealing with as well as providing me with possibilities for joining up these focal dots. I spent a great deal of time mulling over how I could achieve it all, spending time just being in different

ABOVE Evergreen azaleas in the foreground across a serpentine lawn with the white trunks of *Betula utilis* var. *jacquemontii* in the background

spots around the farm and taking in different perspectives throughout the year. There are places in the garden that are favourite spots and views that change with the seasons. In the spring there is the Woodland Garden before the leaves come out, so you can actually look down into it and see the contours of the ground, which are quite extraordinary. I knew I had to bring out the contrast between the formality of 'garden rooms' whilst taking into account the informality and the irregular shape of the land I was working with. There was no way this delicate balance could be achieved through the use of formal hedges so I decided to do it with informal plantings of shrubs and a few trees.

In the end I started joining up my focal dots with a serpentine planting through the middle of the 'old orchard' that provided me with a strong connective thread. I very soon realised that, actually, it is not the shape of the border that matters because what you see is the shape of the lawns. So I altered it all a bit so that the lawns were a pleasing flowing shape while at the same time trying to get the view from an existing cobbled bridge through constructing a ha-ha, taking the thatched house in the distance as the focal point. The ha-ha was originally a hedge, so we got the digger in and took it out. We made the ha-ha quite cheaply, using hollow concrete blocks and then banking up the soil behind them.

When the original house was built in 1927 the builders came across a huge stone that could not be moved by the horses but it gradually got pushed up just out of the way. It was there for ages. My vision was a ha-ha and a Henry Moore statue to complete the desired effect. Of course the statue was way beyond my budget but I did have the stone. It

ABOVE John Hawkins worked with me for thirty-eight years before he sadly became seriously ill. He mowed, weeded and did carpentry and just about any other thing that needed doing. Here he turns his hand to stone walling (his favourite).

FOLLOWING PAGES Looking through the acer underplanted with *Prunus laurocerasus* 'Marbled White' towards the front of the tearoom. The lime green flowering plant in the middle distance is *Alchemilla mollis*: Sally Newcomb

was just a case of moving it from one place to another. The digger managed to lift it up into a borrowed trailer that was lined with railway sleepers on the bottom so we did not damage it. Then it was only a matter of driving up the drive, round the road, across our neighbour's field to finally and triumphantly put the stone in its designated place! We did this over one weekend. John Hawkins, who worked here at the time, came to check our progress on the ha-ha the following Monday. The first thing he said was 'pity they didn't move that old stone while they were at it!' I indignantly told him of my intention to have that stone as a memorial with a plaque on it after I died. It just goes to show – one person's rubbish is another person's treasure.

John Hawkins was such a colourful personality to everyone who knew and worked with him and he left a lasting legacy in Burrow Farm Gardens. He deserves a paragraph dedicated to him here. He arrived at Burrow Farm Gardens through a couple in Axminster who had become informally involved in the garden at Burrow Farm. There are seats in this garden now that are dedicated to this couple, Ted and Kit Hellings. They used to let me use their greenhouse and left me a little bit of money to buy the seats. I knew them because, when they moved to Axminster, they asked me to design their garden. John Hawkins maintained their garden and that is how I met him. One of my main instructions from this couple was 'Don't upset John Hawkins because he is such a valuable find as a gardener and for cutting the lawns and everything'. But John turned out to be such an easy person there was no way you could upset him. He ended up by coming to work at Burrow Farm with me for some of the time as well, and then for three times a week once Ted and Kit had sold up and gone into a home. Ted continued to be quite active. He used to love coming out to the greenhouse and watching me, as well as doing the odd bit of watering, opening up the greenhouse in the morning and closing it at night. Sadly he got to the stage when he could not even manage to do that because he had to nurse his wife. By that time I hadn't the heart to stop visiting them even though I no longer really needed to raise my bedding plants in their greenhouse because I had my own.

At first, as I began to join, connect and weave together separated garden 'dots', I was just digging holes and planting shrubs in grass that I kept roughly mown and grazed. I was particularly interested in foliage from the very beginning, so my thinking was that this planting would provide the background of coloured foliage and texture to the later border, which I saw in my mind's eye as coming in front of them. John Gill,

ABOVE *Primula japonica* in abundance enjoying a damp position in the garden

OPPOSITE *Purple Berberis thunbergii f. atropurpurea* with *Rosa* Bonica and *Melianthus major*: Sally Newcomb

the forester I had worked with on the clay pit, had a mainly tree nursery and those that were misshapen and difficult to sell he donated to me. All my first plantings were those misshapen trees. They chose me rather than me choosing them. After this it became a matter of arranging them. There were a couple of tulip trees and I had been given a few Christmas trees by my husband's aunt, who was also a keen gardener, so I used these for a time as in-fillers with some larch trees to provide the screen and help me see what I was aiming at. Among all these trees were bird cherries and some willows and silver birch, nothing special really apart from the tulip trees and an *Acer ginnala* that gives spectacular autumn colour. Over time I have added several magnolias and *Hoheria sexstylosa*, with a few conifers, to achieve the dense heaviness I was aiming for. To add to the envisioned effect I planted shrubs such as hydrangeas and rhododendrons as focal dots. I knew that, eventually, I wanted a long perennial border

in the foreground but I also knew that would be much more labour intensive so I had to be patient while I developed the spine.

For the first fifteen years I knew I could not even contemplate digging any of the herbaceous borders. Structure always has to come first and planting trees and shrubs is a low maintenance endeavour as long as you keep the ground around them clear and they have the chance to grow up and exclude the grass naturally. Directly you are dealing with bare earth, maintenance shoots up exponentially.

I have collected many magnolias over the years because they do well in the conditions of Burrow Farm Gardens but I do not find their foliage particularly inspiring. They were never 'must haves' for me but 'good doers' that mostly thrive in the conditions of Burrow Farm. I know we are all seduced by new introductions and they are all very tempting but I think it is always worth remembering the 'good doers'. These are the

plants, often indigenous to English gardens that perform stoically year after year. Maybe they never take centre stage at certain times of the season but in their defence I would say they are reliable and work hard, providing the necessary backdrop to the more unfamiliar and often eye-catching newcomers.

I started off by planting three magnolias on my thirtieth birthday and four on my fortieth and then I gave up! Of the three that were my thirtieth birthday present to myself two are still here and one has succumbed. All the fortieth ones have survived. The *Magnolia kobus* in the middle of one of the lawns I actually bought from Veitch's nursery in Exeter, a very old and well-known family concern. Tony, my son, was with me and very small at the time. I actually met Muriel Veitch when I went to get my *Magnolia kobus*. She was the last of the Veitch family to run the nursery. I was very keen to talk to her about the magnolia and its requirements but all she wanted to talk about was Tony. My little curly-headed boy was much more interesting to her than a *Magnolia kobus*. She was quite old by then and it was just before she gave up the nursery; Tony was much more entertaining than my magnolia as far as she was concerned.

Initially, what was going to be lawned was maintained by the small ponies belonging to the children, so I did not even have to mow the existing grass. I tethered them in various places until we had the electric fencing then they grazed all the lawns. Twenty years later I was ready to begin adding herbaceous borders and more intensive maintenance became the order of the day. I have used several different approaches to preparing a new border over the years and have come to the conclusion that the best one, because it works for me, is as follows. If you are dealing with an area that is originally grassed down, first mark out the extremities of the proposed border with canes, then take time to view it from different parts of the garden checking that it is sympathetic with other planting nearby. If you are satisfied that it is, put string or a hosepipe curving around the canes, then remove a 'V' shaped cut out of the turf with a spade or half-moon around the edge. Next, spray off the grass in the centre with a commercial weedkiller.

LEFT Deep blue *Hydrangea macrophylla*: Sally Newcomb

BELOW A sunny border where *Verbena bonariensis* thrives amongst salvias with the grey green foliage of *Melianthus major* providing contrasting definition

Any time after the grass in the centre has started to turn yellow, about one to two weeks after spraying, spread the whole area with well-rotted manure. There have to be some advantages to keeping horses! I have found the problem with rotovating or digging over the whole area, particularly in the autumn, is that the soil becomes looser as the air pockets fill with rainwater and it turns into a soggy morass.

My eagerly anticipated and planned long border is one of the few that is south facing in the gardens so I had to take advantage of that. Many of the plants that flower in the second half of the summer tend to be sun lovers so I had to use mainly salvias, crocosmia, *Diascia*

personata and euphorbias. This border has not been planted all that long, about five years now I would say. Later, on the opposite side to this sunny border, I planted another with quite a lot of *Helleborus orientalis* under two of the twenty-five of the *Acer palmatum* seedlings that I had originally bought. They were a foot high then. They are now much bigger, just ordinary seedlings but they make really good autumn colour.

As I was working on my connections between various parts of the garden and joining the dots I found a variegated euphorbia seedling growing between two paving slabs. I did not know of any variegated euphorbias at the time so thought it needed

ABOVE *Rhododendron williamsianum* with *Acer shirasawanum* 'Aureum' further down the path

FOLLOWING PAGES
Thatched summerhouse with *Ammi visnaga* and the scarlet Papaver (Oriental Group) 'Ladybird', an annual poppy: Sally Newcomb

care. I potted it up, then propagated from it a few years later. I grew on several plants. When I had quite a knowledgeable horticulturalist in the garden, I showed it to him. He did not think there was a variegated *Euphorbia characias* and recommended I think about doing something with it. He told me that the best way of getting people to see it and to find out whether it was unique or not, was to take it up to one of the RHS shows at Westminster and register it for an award. He emphasised that of course I would not get an award because nobody else knew about it but at least the 'right' people would see it. I decided to do just that.

The first problem was the trouble of going up on the train to London because, although Axminster is on the mainline to London, it took hours. The train had to stop at every rural station along the line. It still does. I had my prize specimen plant in a pot, protected in a swing bin, so my second problem was negotiating my plant through crowds of people from Waterloo across to the show. On arrival the next obstacle was the thorny question of whether euphorbia was herbaceous or a shrub. I was advised to enter it in one category only to find out later that it was not the right one, so it went into the other. It was a requirement of entry that the plant was left there for two days and that became my next difficulty. There were no storage facilities so I could not leave my swing bin there. I was left with a day of shopping in London and a rubbish bin to cart around – not very sophisticated – and to add to my woes it was also the time of the IRA bomb scares. Every time I put that wretched bin down to look at anything there were suspicious stares.

When I went back to see the outcome of the show I was told that it had been the plant of the show because there had not been another variegated Euphorbia at that time. I was told I had to keep it really secure because sometimes, when plants are new like that, they are stolen. Having been introduced to the murky world of plant discovery I became very nervous about owning this plant. Coming back on the train there was a 'blackout' and my ridiculous and over-dramatic thoughts ran along the lines of 'Oh my God they are going to steal my euphorbia' and I spent the whole journey cradling my swing bin. People must have thought I was mad. Of course I got it back to the safety of Devon but I did not know what to do with it. You cannot hide it away because it needs water and light so it was a bit nerve-racking for a while.

To take it further I contacted Bressingham Gardens as they were advertising for new

plants. I gave them a call and described my prize possession. Adrian Bloom himself rang me back, which made my day. I was so pleased. We arranged that I should take it up to his nursery in Diss because he had not been able to see it at the show. My brother and sister-in-law came with me and it turned out to be a very memorable day because Alan Bloom was still there and he and Adrian took me all round their Dell Garden. Alan was so lovely. If I admired something, he said 'I will dig you up a bit of that'. He gave me various bits. At the end of the day I said 'I must pay you for these because this is your business' but he said 'after a lifetime in horticulture selling plants to the public, nothing gives me greater pleasure than giving plants to an enthusiast'. I think that was such a lovely saying and I have always remembered it. I signed an exclusive agreement with them to introduce my euphorbia. I was also told to take out plant breeders' rights and Bressingham did that on my behalf, so at least the plant was protected.

Unfortunately, it just so happened to be a very bad time of change for them. I continued paying the fees for quite a few years thinking the breakthrough would be bound to come at any time but nothing happened, even though it was the very first variegated euphorbia. Now there are several others, such as 'Tasmanian Tiger' and 'Silver Swan'. In the end I decided enough was enough and waived the royalties whereupon it was immediately propagated and imported from Holland, but not in huge quantities. It appears just occasionally in publications, still called *Euphorbia* 'Burrow Silver', but not making a fortune. In fact, I should say it's probably made a loss, but it's been a wonderful experience along the way!

Euphorbia 'Burrow Silver' seems to have made a comeback recently and is now more readily available. Without DNA testing I can't know whether Tasmanian Tiger is related to it. Maybe or maybe not; I will never find out.

Chapter 4

From a Shady Pergola Walk to a Mediterranean Garden with a Twist: The Rose Garden

LEFT The pergola as it was originally with the Shy Maiden statue

RIGHT The ornamental gates at the end of the path in the Rose Garden with *Rosa* 'American Pillar' climbing in the background: Sue Deere

In summer, what we used to call the Pergola Walk became a favourite place. We now call it the Rose Garden or Mediterranean Garden. This area started as an oblong little paddock with small jumps that the children used for riding.

We had some old chairs that we wanted to get rid of so John Hawkins took them to the tip. He came back saying masses of stone slabs had been dumped there and he thought I could do something with them. I immediately went to cast my eye over them. It turned out they were the old paving slabs from the streets of Ottery St Mary that had been replaced. We borrowed a tractor and trailer and went

up to the tip, a journey of some distance, and asked how much they wanted for the slabs. It was decided we could have them for so much a ton. We asked if they had a weigh-bridge so we could weigh them but of course they didn't so we filled up the tractor twice and that was the start of the paving through the middle of the Pergola Walk.

At about that time I had the opportunity to go skiing with my brother and sister-in-law. I had to choose between the holiday and making this new area of garden. Typically I thought the Pergola Walk would leave a legacy that would last far longer than a skiing holiday, so I put the money into that.

ABOVE Path through the
Mediterranean Garden
with *Veronica gentianoides*
and forget-me-nots
providing the blue
splashes of colour

RIGHT *Hydrangea paniculata* 'Limelight' to the left with *Lobelia* 'Hadspen Purple', *Lythrum* 'Firecandle' and umbels of the purple *Angelica* 'Vicar's Mead' in the foreground providing a restful colour combination and echoing the shape of the hydrangea

FOLLOWING PAGES Melianthus major providing the architectural foliage on the right. *Agastache* 'Purple Haze' with pink annual *Cosmos bipinnatus*: Sally Newcomb

I never did go skiing, not then or later – the hammock repeated!

We decided on a sort of wooden structure to make the pergola and that lasted quite a few years, but I am never very good at controlling climbers. I grew wisteria, clematis and vine in a repeated planting pattern, as well as *Akebia quinata* that is rampant and of course went berserk. I started by trying to keep the centre of the pergola open but pruning when you are standing on the ground is one thing, pruning up a six-foot ladder is another. The whole thing got very top heavy and really shady underneath and this made it quite difficult to grow other plants. When the gales came sweeping in from the sea some years later they blew the pergola down. We took that as a sign and decided to remove what was left of it. The whole area suddenly became a really sunny and sheltered oasis with the beech hedge that had grown up around it so I decided to transform it into a Mediterranean garden. To enhance the Mediterranean feel we built some impressive stone pillars and wrought iron gates for the entrance.

Because of this piece of serendipity I was able to completely change the planting to summer flowering plants instead of shade lovers. It was definitely a change for the better because there are lots of shady areas throughout the garden as we have so many trees. It gave me a chance to try a new gardening experience and presented me with a different and appealing challenge. For the first time I had somewhere that was really sunny to play with. I colour themed the border with pinks and blues and silvers and I have made every attempt to keep to the scheme since, even though it has not always been as easy as it seems. You have to go with the conditions and the plants that will thrive and this inevitably limits the palette and is not as easy as painting a picture. Another lesson learnt!

ABOVE One of the oil jars in the Mediterranean Garden surrounded by the purple foliage of *Angelica* 'Vicar's Mead' which self sows generously throughout the garden

To enhance the Mediterranean feel, over the years I bought six oil jars of various sizes and we planted six squares of box hedging to surround each jar, to give focal points of interest and draw the eye. As the hedges grow taller we raise the jars on bricks to retain the impression that the jars are supported on top of the box hedging squares. I am pleased with the result because, to my eyes, this design technique adds interest on each side as you walk down the central path. There are just two small, slow-growing trees in this garden, a pink flowered *Robinia hispida* (the Rose Acacia) and in the far corner, a fern leaved purple beech, *Fagus sylvatica* 'Rohanii'.

I have introduced many roses to this garden, mainly pink, white and crimson ground cover roses – some of the County series. Lancashire and Sussex provide the flower carpet and then I have the larger *Rosa* Bonica. *Melianthus major* has created large groups of glaucous foliage and I have used Cardoons for a silvery contrast. *Eupatorium atropurpurea* has been used for its bold purple flowers in midsummer and because it attracts swarms of butterflies and bees. Other plants associated in this garden are *Lobelia* 'Hadspen Purple, *Lythrum salicaria* 'Firecandle', *Physostegia virginiana* 'Vivid' and *Nepeta* 'Walker's Low'. I leave one or two small areas for annuals

BELOW Spring in the Mediterranean Garden with mauve tulips setting off the terracotta of the oil jars. There is a variegated *Acer platanoides* 'Drummondii' in the top left of the picture and *Populus alba* with its silvery foliage placed to the right

such as cosmos, godetia or *Cerinthe purpurea*. At the end of the Rose Garden is one of my 'sorbet areas'. I use these as a convenient connecting device between intense patches of vivid plant colour. They are very neutral, calming and green, a palette cleanser for the eyes before you enter the next block of vibrant colour.

I have also tried to introduce tulips to this garden but, however hard I try to fence it off from marauding rabbits and deer, there is always the odd time they get, in wreaking havoc and causing mayhem, especially with the tulips. They seem to make a bee-line for them.

Very recently we have had two pairs of rather splendid wrought iron gates placed at either end of the grass walkway on the perimeter of this garden. They present quite a challenge as they need to be deer-proof while allowing tractor access and clearance. Fingers crossed – we shall see.

Chapter 5

From Washing Lines to Terraces: The Terrace Garden

LEFT The summerhouse in the Terrace Garden with the scarlet *Dahlia* 'Garden Wonder' and blue agapanthus. The grass in the top left is *Chionochloa conspicua* that originates from New Zealand

For ages the area that is now the Terrace Garden was where John had his vegetable garden and my washing line was there too because it was close to the house. There is also a hut that we've always called 'the kennel' because we used to put lots of straw in there for the dogs and use it as a place to dry them off and provide shelter for the waifs and strays that have turned up at Burrow Farm over the years we've been here. When we bought the farm this was actually described in the property details as accommodation suitable for a single man. I think this was because long before our time at Burrow Farm a single man, who had been a prisoner of war, had actually been assigned this converted chicken house to live in. The area that was to become the Terrace Garden also became home to a number of our 'waifs and strays'. That converted chicken shed has assumed multiple guises through all our years here and before we arrived, from accommodation suitable for a single man, to a kennel for a motley crew of dogs, to our children's playroom, and it is still there in the Terrace Garden today. I think the first stray to take up residence was a Greyhound we named Jill. She adopted John Hawkins as a 'friend' and must have left a sign at the bottom of the drive saying 'all homeless dogs and strays welcome here, kind and understanding family and highly desirable accommodation'.

Another time, a black collie arrived out of the blue one evening at the house. We reported this to the police who asked if we would keep it until someone claimed it. I agreed but I told the family not to feed this dog, not to play with it and not to encourage it in any way. By the morning it had worn a track round the house so we let it in and all my 'nots' went out of the window. About six months later the police rang asking about 'that dog we had'. I told them we still had it and were looking after it for them as promised. At that time you used to need licences for dogs so I didn't really consider him to be mine, but in the end he stayed with us forever. We called him Sammy Davis Junior and he was with us until, tragically, he got run over. From the very beginning of his life here he became very attached to Sue-Sue but when she went to live abroad he attached himself to me.

After Sammy Davis died we went to the RSPCA and got another dog, also black because he reminded us of Davis. They told us this replacement dog was a persistent stray. We called him Smith. He seemed to settle in with us very happily but he was a 'master thief' – he could open any door and as soon as it got to dusk each day he would just melt away and be gone. Later on he would return but you would worry about what he was doing in the meantime. Apparently he used to visit our neighbours, open their door, eat their cat's food, and then go and lie down in front of their fire. I am sure they must have encouraged him. He would also go down into the village looking for mischief. If you took your eye off him for a second he was gone. It was a real problem.

One evening Smith did his usual disappearing act but we didn't worry unduly because we thought he would return as usual. Anyway, by morning he hadn't appeared and when he still failed to turn up I rang the police. They said somebody had found a dog fitting his description and they gave me a contact telephone number. I thanked them, but when I took down the number they laughed and said to me 'Do you know the local area for this number?' I said 'No'. It turned out to be Eastbourne in East Sussex. Apparently, a coach driver had spotted him on a dangerous corner of the A35. The driver stopped and encouraged him into the coach to keep him out of danger and then contacted the police in Axminster. When he phoned them they said they had no available dog handler on duty so the driver would have to take him home or put him out where he was. The driver said he'd already driven three or

four miles from where he picked him up and couldn't possibly leave him so far from that spot, so he took him home. When I rang the next day to arrange to go and get him from his newly adopted family, they said not to worry because he was so lovely and friendly. I was concerned though because he was such an escape artist and I thought he might get out and not know where he was. I went to get him and found out that in the three days he spent in his temporary home, he taught their labrador to open doors too.

Anyway, that is enough of dogs. While we were developing this area of garden, the rest of the garden was maturing and so were the children. Our daughter Penny was undecided about what she wanted to do after she left school so I went to look round Bicton College for her. The upshot of that was my discovery that there were several 'mature' students on one of their horticultural courses. So I signed up for one myself. After three years studying there for one day a week I took City and Guilds Amenity Horticulture. Probably my

ABOVE The summerhouse
in the Terrace Garden
with *Fuchsia magellanica*
'alba aureovariegata' and
Hydrangea 'Limelight'

floral marquee or on an outside stand. The
whole enterprise entails a huge amount of
time and dedication from the whole team of
our 'extended garden family'. It is great fun
doing it and always inspiring to hear people's
comments as they look round the stand.
Over the years I have come up with a tried
and tested formula to create each exhibit. I
do a basic design a few weeks before, usually
on the back of an envelope or any old scrap
paper. The next step is to go round both my
own nursery and Tony's nursery a few days
before setting up the display to see what
plants are looking good at the time and pull
them out to take down to the show. At this
point it becomes obvious what the colour
scheme will be for the various areas of the
show garden. It is very important to select
those plants that will grow in the particular
conditions that can be found in a natural
garden – shade loving plants amongst the
trees and moisture lovers beside the pond.
I have a collection of 'knick knacks' that I
put to use in the display – a small garden
seat, a little old lawn mower, a garden trug
and old tools. A small wooden wheelbarrow
that belonged to my grandfather often takes
pride of place. We also have bits and pieces of
wooden fencing and a door and window that
my husband, John made up into what looks
like a house, or sometimes a potting shed, or
even a boathouse according to the theme for
that year. We've been judged 'Best in Show'
several times.

The shelter that also now graces the
Terrace Garden was originally built of trellis
but the climbers on it were so vigorous that,
after a few years, the weight of them caused
it to collapse. We replaced it with a more
substantial structure of stone with a rosemary
tile roof. The pillars on the corners are more
of the grave edging stones that were recycled
from a cemetery through a landscaping
commission of Tony's. Some of them bear
relevant messages like 'rest in peace' and one
says 'peace after great pain'!

proudest achievement was a Distinction in
Horticultural Machinery – purely theoretical
I hasten to add!

I think the value of taking a course like
that is that you have to study the whole
syllabus and not just concentrate on the parts
that interest you most. I was not particularly
interested in bedding schemes at the time but
found the knowledge I gained useful when
I later did commercial planting for housing
companies and when I began to design and
set up the show gardens that began to take up
more of my time.

I have been doing show gardens as part of
the Axe Vale Show since its inception, about
twenty-five years ago now. My involvement
is to design and build gardens, either in the

ABOVE Gravel path through the Terrace Garden highlighting the yellow border with *Fuchsia magellanica* var. *molinae* 'Alba Aureovariegata', *Hydrangea* 'Limelight' and *Lycesteria* 'Golden Lanterns'. The solid shape of the Buxus contrasts with the filigree foliage surrounding it. *Helianthus* 'Lemon Queen' also makes a statement on the right of the path

As far as the planting in the Terrace Garden goes, there are fastigiate *Pyrus calleryana* 'Chanticleer' trees interspersed with antique rhubarb forcers, forming a semi-circle. The borders are planted with mainly cottage type perennials such as campanulas, *Diascia personata*, *Papaver orientalis* and paeonies with variegated honesty that happily seeds itself throughout. From the shelter round to the left the colour scheme runs from white to pink to crimson at the far end. From the right and running in the opposite direction it moves from cream to yellow to orange. Some blue campanula, catmint and honesty are used to unite the two sides. A large planting of *Chamaenerion angustifolium* 'Album' makes a fine feature in the summer months. It can be a little invasive so be warned!

Another eye-catching structure in our Terrace Garden, beside the multi-purpose 'chicken shed', is the rather large and eye-catching obelisk we built in a prominent position there. The pinnacle of this obelisk came from a Victorian hotel outside Bridport that was being demolished. In the process, any bits of carved stone and things like that were sold off. The particular type of pinnacle that had caught my eye at the sale had started life as the top of a Victorian window and there also were several similar stone items. I bought that particular one as well as some of the other pieces of stone, now incorporated into one of the bridges in the gardens. When I bought that pinnacle I admit I had no idea what I was going to do with it but I knew immediately that it had found a home as we built a column 'thing' out of all sorts of random pieces of carved stone, collected over the years. Building that focal point for the Terrace Garden was really quite difficult

ABOVE Looking up the steps to the obelisk
which in reality is more imposing than the
picture seems to suggest. *Rosa* 'Paul's Himalayan
Musk' meanders gracefully over a wooden
frame to the right. The white rose in the
foreground is one of the County Roses to be
found throughout the garden. This one is *Rosa*
Kent = 'Poulcov'. To the top of the picture
is *Cornus* 'Norman Haddon' a prolifically
flowering dogwood with flowers followed by red
strawberry like fruits

BELOW The armillary sundial our children gave us for our Golden Wedding Anniversary with the summerhouse in the background. The pillars were constructed from re-cycled grave edging stones, some of which still bear their inscriptions

RIGHT Purple and white honesty with *Narcissus* 'Thalia' and forget-me-nots

because we had a variety of bits of stone from my pile of potentially useful materials (PUMS), and then fitted them together, cemented them and tied string round them as they set. That gave us the column but then we had the problem of trying to figure out how on earth we were going to get the pinnacle on top. In the end we constructed a tripod of poles with a pulley at the top. We managed to winch it up there with the help of a lot of people, get it into position, and then cement it.

My collection of random pieces of carved stone had been growing for years and started partly with the idea of building a new house to replace the 'rustic accommodation' we had first lived in when we bought the farm. They were 'stored' in an organically growing

pile out in the field and optimistically called 'Mary's house'. There were heaps of wood and stone because we both knew the original dwelling, being an asbestos bungalow, was not going to last forever. We lived in that bungalow for about thirty-two years and then built the house we are in now. The idea was to build something substantial and we have now been in this house since October 1994. It only took us three decades to get here!

The central feature of our Terrace Garden now is an armillary sundial, a present from our children to celebrate and mark our Golden Wedding anniversary. It's in an appropriate location as the Terrace Garden runs along the side of the drive leading to the main entrance of the 'new' house.

LEFT A blue clematis that prefers to act as ground cover rather than climb the tree behind it: Sally Newcomb

RIGHT *Echium vulgare* 'Blue Bedder', *Ammi visnaga* and the scarlet *Penstemon* 'Firebird': Sally Newcomb

Chapter 6

From a Lead Planter a Whole Garden Flows: The Millennium Garden

The idea of the Millennium Garden started when I went up to The Chelsea Flower Show in 1998 and saw a lovely lead planter with the year 2000 engraved on it. The millennium was going to be a big event for most of us; everyone was speculating where they would be and what they were going to be doing when the chimes struck. Well, I of course got carried away on this wave of collective desire to make the event something to remember and I put down a deposit on the eye catching lead planter. The millennium was, in all honesty, the ultimate excuse for something I wanted so badly and quite simply had to own. In common with others who have made similar spontaneous and wildly extravagant purchases, my thoughts on the train home were far more sobering. I had spent rather a lot of money on something I had no idea where to 'place' in the garden. On the other hand I was sure I was not the first, and would not be the last, to have to explain away my indulgence to others when I got home.

I carried that planter around in my mind's eye, trying to find the right space to display it to its full advantage. The solution of course was another 'land grab'. I decided I had to make a separate garden that would show off my new acquisition to its greatest advantage and it would be called the Millennium Garden. In my mind this was also a justifiable excuse because for some time, ever since I had seen the rills at Hestercombe and Coleton Fishacre, I had wanted to construct one.

What had stopped me doing this previously was that I could never quite envisage where, or whether, there was a right place in the existing garden. Of course the solution was to combine these two wishes, the planter and the rill, and gradually the idea grew and began to coalesce.

I decided to develop a piece of land I had already started working. Before my designs for a rill had even taken shape, John Hawkins and I had begun to build a wall along the bottom of the nursery. As we built it, I can remember getting about three quarters of the way along and stopping because it all seemed a little bit final. I knew myself very well, so well that instead of putting a wall right the way through I decided to leave a little gap in the middle with the idea that it could be adapted as a doorway and accommodate any possible future expansion. For several years we just had a fence panel propped over this gap.

Now I think about it, I have to admit that, even before that, John Gill, the forester who helped me so much in the beginning, also had a hand in structuring this garden because one day, out of the blue, he sent over about fifty *Chamaecyparis lawsoniana* which had been blown and bent by the wind and then allowed to grow up, so they were all in a sort of half-moon shape. They suddenly arrived one breakfast time because John was only too well aware of my reputation as a 'rescue home' for plants as well as animals. He knew that if he or anyone else said 'could you do anything

with this?', I always said yes – I still do.

Anyway, I had to think quickly about what I was going to do with these distorted cupressus and decided to make a wind break out of them that would run right down through the garden. We have a southerly wind that blows in from the sea and this wind tends to barrel through the garden in the summer. The idea was that a line of cupressus trees would break it up a bit and I can admit that the boundary of the Millennium Garden was one of my plant rescue missions. Michael, my grandson who is now responsible for managing the garden, still curses these cupressus because they are quite high as well as wide, making them difficult to cut, and of course we do have to keep them trimmed. Half have now had to be removed because they became so huge that they encroached on the space behind the adjacent netting tunnel and were making the kitchen of the tearoom very dark.

One solution inevitably leads to another problem down the line. When I started thinking about my design for the Millennium Garden to be sited on the other side of this windbreak, I realised I had a major issue to deal with. The problem was that I wanted to design a more formal garden with straight lines but the straight lines had to tie up with existing structures such as the established *Chamaecyparis lawsoniana* windbreak and this boundary was not at right angles with the wall we had built. The proposed three quarters of an acre plot was consequently a slightly weird shape. It took me some time to think how I could get over this particularly knotty problem as the wall at the bottom of the nursery that would form another of the boundaries was not wide enough for the proposed plot of the Millennium Garden. My genius solution was to build a summerhouse out beyond the location of the nursery that I could then take and incorporate into the width of the Millennium Garden.

Having got over my width problem I then had the 'not at right angles' difficulty, which gave me the additional headache of lining up the rill with what was to be the doorway in the gap I had left in our wall, where the fence panel was 'temporarily' propped. I knew that doorway would have to be my centre line and then all the other measurements would have to come off that. If nothing else, this formal garden had to give the illusion of straight lines. I also knew that the lawns coming off the rill could not be anything other than straight, whereas the borders, even if they tapered once planted, could at least give the illusion of 'straightness'. Having sorted out fundamental issues such as these, it all began to fall into place.

An additional difficulty was that the plot was steeply sloping so we had to build a retaining wall at the bottom and hire a digger

to cut and fill around a centre line where the nepeta and wisterias are now. We dug the soil out and put it behind the wall until we had levelled out the two areas at the top and bottom of the plot and then the steps went in the middle. All this was extremely time consuming and expensive but I also had the confidence that this was money well spent and I would reach the point where I had the intuitive feeling that it was 'right'.

That feeling of 'rightness' is not something you can easily explain. All you can say to others planning similar big projects is that suddenly you just 'know' what is going to work – not very helpful I suppose. We actually had to lower the first half of the area by making 'sort of trenches' at the top where we were going to have some of the retaining walls. These retaining walls also had to be built before large amounts of soil were moved, making it all a matter of working

ABOVE Planting a magnolia to celebrate the Millennium trees with Sue-Sue's children, my grandchildren, Alice and James. We were helped, of course, by two collies, Dollie and Isca

with the weather. John Hawkins just could not see or visualise these underground walls and I had to keep explaining them to him. He had never had to build walls in a trench before! The lawns were placed once we had levelled everything off. Tony, my son, always has bits of turf left over from his landscaping commissions so we used all the off-cuts and turf bits and laid them out like a jigsaw. John Hawkins was particularly good at this.

Once I had worked everything out structurally, the planting was not so difficult because I had a robust theme. I asked each member of the family to plant a shrub there for the Millennium, from our children to their children. The idea was they would each plant something different. Most of the magnolias were planted this way, and the wisterias. Tony had a large *Cornus controversa* 'Variegata' in a crate that he had dug up from a previous landscaping development. He decided it was much too good to throw away. It had spent years being ferried backwards and forwards to the Axminster Festival where it had a star role so he felt it had done its duty and should be retired gracefully. We released it from its crate and into the new Millennium Garden it went. Penny, my garden designer daughter, wanted something special but was so picky about what she wanted I am not sure she actually got to plant anything. Penny's children, Mark and Michael, also planted

magnolias, one of which is still there, and Michael says it's his, but the other one went. Jane and her family planted the wisterias. Her two children planted the purple ones across the middle, and Jane planted the white one down at the bottom of the garden.

Sue-Sue, my third daughter, planted *Magnolia* 'Susan' and her children each planted a different variety. Her son Peter, who at the time was really tiny, about 18 months old, planted *Magnolia x veitchii* 'Peter Veitch'. Penny's son, David, planted *Acer davidii* that actually succumbed as well. You don't have success with everything.

As I said, the main inspiration for the design of the rill came from Hestercombe and Coleton Fishacre augmented by odd pictures in books and magazines. To construct the rill we put a butyl liner down underneath all the stonework, the idea being that as the water was going to be circulated we had to be very careful not to lose any on the way. Obviously some is lost from evaporation but otherwise we knew there could not be any leaks. Paving slabs went on the top of the liner as well. The electricity for the pump came from digging across from the pump house that serves the nearby swimming pool on a time switch. Most of the time we do not have to worry about it but sometimes we suddenly become aware it has stopped and the water is not running. Then we have to get the hosepipe and blow everything back. Michael is getting to be quite the expert in doing that.

For the Millennium Garden I had a colour theme for the borders running down each side. On the left hand side going down it was going to be silver, pinks and blues. On the right hand side it was yellows and blues so, structurally, I have the hypericum on that right side and also the box hedging round the seats that I bought with my 'inheritance' from Ted and Kit Hellings. Nineteen years later it is still basically like that. I did not want the borders in this garden to look too contrived and to achieve this I have learnt

that if you thread into each border some of the same colour from the opposite border, you can achieve the hoped for sense of formal 'informality'. In the Millennium Garden, having blue on both sides achieves that balance.

As I have mentioned, I also had the problem of the conifer hedge running along one side. The land tends to slope down away from this hedge which meant that, to level it up visually, I had to have height on the opposite side and, to achieve the required height here, I planted quite tall things at the back. I went for several different conifers with a yellow theme. I used *Chamaecyparis lawsoniana* and the golden *Acer pseudoplatanus* 'Worleei', like a golden leaved sycamore, that is quite tall. Then I also planted an orange flowered berberis that I grew from seed. It is probably a cross but very showy, proving the value of experimenting and growing

plants from your own seed. These plants act as the solid boundary. I also have *Elaeagnus ebbingei*, a good, dense, evergreen shrub with a wonderful scent. You can hardly see the flowers at all on this shrub but I often walk down there trying to identify the source of the heavenly smell and then of course realise it is the *Elaeagnus ebbingei*. The flowers are so tiny, borne in the axils of the leaf, but give such wonderful scent in the autumn. Above all else it was essential that the planting for the Millennium Garden should help to frame the wonderful views out to the countryside beyond. I am satisfied it achieves that.

One corner of the plot had been used for years as a nursery bed so there were a few existing plants I wanted to keep that had to be accommodated in my plan. One of these, the weeping ash, was a bit of a problem because again it meant the soil levels were all wrong. Instead of trying to level it all out my solution

BELOW The old door between the Millennium Garden and the nursery in a froth of *Erigeron karvinskianus*: Jo Whitworth

RIGHT Looking through the circular window in the summerhouse to the top of the Millennium Garden with *Salvia forsskaolii*: Sally Newcomb

was to make a raised circular bed so it looked as though these plants were meant to be there. There is a *Betula utilis* var. *jacquemontii* that is original and also a *Viburnum carlesii* 'Aurora' near the steps, all quite big and well-established but in fact just happy accidents and happen-chance.

Half way down the Millennium Garden are the two *Wisteria sinensis* 'Prolific' which I always had in mind to prune down as shrubs and in this way keep the whole garden open so you can see the view looking over the valley. They act as visual cues between the doorway and the bottom of the garden beyond the rill.

The idea is that the view from the bottom looks back at the doorway and then you look from the doorway out the other way along the rill to the valley beyond.

I always wanted the doorway to be an archway. I found three old planks at a reclamation yard and drew a picture of what I wanted it to look like. I took it to Peter Addie, just up the road, who put it together. I did not want a high finish on it; I wanted it to look really old. We had a couple of old genuine strap gate hinges that I gave to him to put on as well. John Hawkins and I made the arch and came up with all sorts of concoctions to prop it up during the construction that tested our building skills to the limit. How did they manage huge viaducts and bridges in the past?

The summerhouse that solved my width problem was designed to have two walls at the back and a pillar at the front. I had gone to

a reclamation yard in Herefordshire and seen five lovely stone pillars. They must have been so pleased when I came along and wanted one and they seemed quite happy to deliver it down here! The stone floor with a circle of terracotta pots in the middle was again inspired by a visit to Hestercombe and we made two circular windows at the back. John Hawkins loved building straight walls but he did not like fiddly bits. He told me straight that if I wanted 'fiddly bits' like that, I could do them myself and he would do the rest. I found a small motor tyre that had come off a piece of farm machinery, placed it where I wanted a window to be and then built round it. The minute I took the tyre out each time was heart stopping – will it collapse, won't it – but of course once you have it complete it holds itself. I had to do that four times, inside and outside. I also had some nice tiles in my PUMS collection that had been there for a few years, so into the summerhouse they went.

John Hawkins and I made a good team.

He loved building but never wanted to see the plans. He did all the stonework and I did the pointing and what he decided were the 'fiddly bits'. I learnt quite early on that you have either got to do these things yourself or pay someone else to do them for you, so I developed my skills out of necessity. It was always John Hawkins that did the main part. He had an amazingly straight eye even though he had to battle with the sloping ground. We often used to forget to take the spirit level onto the site but we always used to carry on and plan to get the spirit level after lunch. We ended up building the whole summerhouse without a spirit level ever making it down there.

The infamous lead planter went in to the garden fairly early on because it was the inspiration for the whole enterprise. The planting in it is changed every year but we usually have some tulips in it. I have found over the years that the deer put the Millennium Garden at the top of their itinerary. They visit us very regularly in this

RIGHT A restful seat in the Millennium Garden with *Campanula lactiflora* providing the focal points against a backdrop of mature trees: Jo Whitworth

part of the gardens and they are devils for eating tulips. Through much trial and error I have learnt that if you plant enough daffodils between the tulips that tends to put them off because daffodils are poisonous. My favourite tulip is probably Spring Green and I plant that with *Narcissus* 'Thalia' in between and hope the deer have a problem sorting out the tulips from the daffodils. When these die down, we put in the summer bedding, things like diascias and pelargoniums but that changes each year according to my fancy at the time.

Container planting really is about the art of remembering to water and feed regularly. I try and concentrate the pots in parts of the garden that are not far from a water source and those in the Millennium Garden are all easily accessible from the nursery water supply.

As there was so much structure built into the design of the Millennium Garden it looked quite good from the very beginning. To my mind it began to look 'right' when the planting on the right hand side that was mostly new, balanced what was on the left, including the hedge. Until then it looked a

little as though it was falling off sideways. The lawn always looked level but it took some time to get the planting in perspective and rectify the 'visual tilt' by balancing the visual weight from all possible viewpoints from either side. I usually achieve these visual corrections with denser evergreens that put extra weight in those places that appear to be sloping down and somehow seem to make everything look more balanced. Of course, the trick is to also be able to select plants for the conditions that suit them. Now, as the Millennium Garden has matured on the yellow side we have the height right and those plants are suited to the additional shade because yellow foliage plants tend to thrive in those conditions.

The sunny border of the Millennium Garden provides just the right conditions for silvery plants like the *Astelia*, a New Zealand plant rather like a *Phormium* but grey leaved, which provided a structural basis for this border along with the several magnolias, Michaelmas daises and Shasta daisies (*Leucanthemum* × *superbum*). I planted the *Leucanthemum* under the white-stemmed birch, *Betula utilis* var. *jacquemontii*, and I

ABOVE *Erigeron karvinskianus* and *Leucanthemum vulgare* enjoying the gravel area at the top of the Millennium Garden

I designed the pond for the rill with a formal shelf about six inches below the water level so that I could stand pots on it. That way, if the water did drop right down, it would still look good visually. In fact the water level does not drop that much because the pond contains such a large volume of water but that calculation was far beyond me. Two of the corners have got permanent planting but I stand seasonal things in terracotta pots on the other two corners. Plants like *Iris ensata* work well when they are in flower and also *Lobelia cardinalis* that is inclined to be total slug fodder in a garden but not when immersed in water. I also have some Arum lilies and insectivorous plants in pots. I think these can all probably survive the winter but just to be on the safe side I take them into a cold greenhouse. We have had to net the pond because of the herons that are attracted to the large fish population darting around a vigorous water lily placed in the centre.

The Millennium Garden is a particularly popular part of the garden with visitors. The secret of its success, I think, is that I had to plan everything in detail for such a long time because we didn't have the labour or the money to do it all instantly. As it turned out, this garden is an important addition to Burrow Farm Gardens, not only because it is a celebration garden and has that exuberance about it, but also because it has a formality that is quite different from anywhere else.

Thinking back, I realise that my guilty conscience over the expense of the planter is nothing compared to what I should feel about the cost of creating the quarter of an acre garden that became necessary to accommodate it! However, I also know I am not the first gardener, and nor will I be the last, to succumb to a whim and then be faced with the headache of turning a spontaneous purchase into a lengthy period of creativity.

love the combination. The blue in this border is provided by the drifts of nepeta in various places, including in the middle under the wisteria. *Diascia personata* is also a good 'doer' in this border – I find it is very satisfactory – and two roses, *Rosa* 'Hertfordshire', one at the top and one near the bottom, provide a nice single rose which is a bright magenta pink. It is described as a ground cover rose but in reality it grows to about four feet high. The only colour combination I really do not like is pink and yellow, but providing they are segregated and they have each got something else, like blue, with them, they are absolutely fine. Unfortunately there is one area in this border that is quite steep. And I have a devil of a job with the rabbits scratching everything out as well!

Chapter 7

From Nought to Fifty: The Grasses Garden

LEFT Bark path winding through the Grasses Garden. *Miscanthus* 'Morning Light' can be seen to the left. The borders to each side of the path are dotted with bright splashes of crocosmia

The Grasses Garden was created to celebrate fifty years of hard work. By this time Burrow Farm Gardens was giving pleasure to an increasing number of visitors, as well as to the gardeners working in it, so everybody kept saying 'what are you going to do to commemorate fifty years?' Well of course, with my track record it had to be a new bit of garden.

The previous autumn, a nursery up at Rousden had ceased trading and over a period of several months had been trying to sell its remaining stock. I made them an offer to clear all the plants that were left. Amongst this clearance stock there turned out to be a very high percentage of grasses, possibly because grasses do not have an immediate appeal when people are choosing plants and certainly do not have that 'buy me' wow factor when seen in a plastic pot. I tried selling them myself in the nursery here the following year but very few of them sold, so I decided to put them to good use. I am usually immune to garden trends unless I feel they fit in with the overall philosophy behind Burrow Farm Gardens and its development. I know some things just would not fit, for example a parterre or knot garden, because they are so formal and, apart from anything else, it is quite difficult to create one of these on sloping ground. That sort of garden was never an option for a celebration garden here. Prairie style planting using grasses is, I know, currently very fashionable in garden

design but, as in a lot of other places in Burrow Farm, my grasses were more of a rescue mission and so, yet again, through this mixture of serendipity and planning rather than the influence of any garden fashion, the Grasses Garden began to take shape in my mind.

Having made the decision for a grasses garden that would extend the season for the gardens as a whole I wanted to create that certain look and flow I had found to be missing in other grasses gardens I had visited. I wanted to make it so you really walked down in and through the area, with the grasses waving above you, so you viewed the planting from below rather than on a level. The first thing I did was to hire a digger and excavate a sort of curving path through the middle of the site. We threw up the soil to left and right, making mounds on either side of a now sunken path, so that as people walked through they would get the full effect of grasses whispering as the breezes blew through them and would experience the sinuous and graceful movement of these plants, in this way creating an echo of the sea that is so close by. To build up the sides of these mounds we put a lot of old soil and manure and everything else we could find that would help to achieve this effect and then we put a drain through the middle so it did not get too wet. Everything went from there really.

The site itself is very exposed to the winds that sweep across the valley but grasses are

ABOVE A sea of grass.
Looking up through the
Grasses Garden between
the two stone pillars. Deep
pink sedums, pale yellow
nasturtiums and *Aster
amellus* 'King George'
provide eye-catching glints
of colour: Nicola Stocken

at their best in these conditions. It is what they are meant for. The movement and the sound are simultaneously mesmerising to the eye and spectacular to the ear, mimicking the wave-like motion of the sea I'd hoped to achieve.

There are grasses for all conditions but the majority need full sun. The proposed site was ideal because it gets full sun all the way round and throughout the day. With grasses I have found that if you plant them with one side in sun and the other in shade they grow out towards the sun and the next thing you know, they have flopped. They need as much sun and overhead direct light as you can provide them with. I did not want this garden to be grasses only and I wanted to focus on making it into a garden that is at the height of its glory in August and September, before the autumn colour gradually reaches a crescendo in the rest of the gardens. Grasses are ideal for this. I also knew I should concentrate on asters, sedums, persicarias and plants that

flower and reach their zenith at the end of the season. A planting, to my mind, is not complete without a few self-seeding plants weaving their way between those that have been purposefully placed. Solid groups of plants with *Verbena bonariensis* fulfil this wish to perfection. On this note of self-seeding, I would say that grasses are lovely in the winter with the frost sparkling on them or hung with the diamond necklaces provided by the Devon mists, but beware – some of them will self-sow and there is nothing more difficult than weeding out unwanted grass seedlings in a grasses garden! Colour-wise, it followed that the grasses garden ended up being mostly pinks and mauves because everything was dictated by the plants chosen for their seasonal appeal and suitability for the prevailing conditions of the garden. I have always been interested in colour palettes, possibly because I was a child of the Second World War when the outsides of all crayons were just plain wood. After the war,

when crayons were produced with coloured outsides and displayed as a harmonious wheel of varying shades, I just loved them. I can remember standing in Woolworths looking at all the colours and being completely entranced by them.

It's lucky that my rescue grasses were all well labelled because my knowledge of grass nomenclature was limited. Inevitably of course, some of the labels went missing in transit and so began my grasses education. I really knew very little about grasses other than that I liked a few and already grew these in other parts of the garden, but that was it. I admit I am still not very knowledgeable about nomenclature because there are just so many of them and, to my eye, the subtlety of their differences makes them quite indistinguishable. I am beginning to recognise what is going to be a miscanthus and what is going to be a pennisetum but I am not an authority at all. Like a lot of gardeners, I muddle through, putting together combinations that are pleasing to the eye, or to mine at least, and there are the inevitable mistakes as I go along but that is the joy of gardening.

There are some beautiful prairie gardens with exceptional planting, but I think these gardens have to be fairly extensive in size to make an impression. I did not have the luxury of such a large expanse at Burrow Farm so I had to supplement it with other ideas and make the appropriate tweaks. I planned a little bit more structure in my Grasses Garden by using two groups of upright conifers. Initially, I felt the area was too flat, with no structure to it, so as well as the mounds I planted these conifers at a very early stage in my development of the plot. Also, I thought that this would mean that when the grasses were all cut down there would at least be something to draw the eye at other times of the year. I planted about five upright conifers, supplemented by a few other trees and shrubs at the back. The five upright conifers are

Thuja occidentalis 'Holmstrup' and there are also one or two flowering cornuses and one or two buddleias that flower at the right time.

The development of this garden sounds very trouble free. I had the plants, access to the digger, a plan in my head and it all seemed to come together quite seamlessly, but of course there is no place for that sort of smugness amongst gardeners. One of the problems I had was that the soil I brought in to build up the mounds hid a whole lot of Montbretia, *Crocosmia x crocosmiiflora* corms that I have been trying to deal with ever since. I have purposely planted some crocosmia down the centre of the garden but not the plain orange ones that thrive in the Devon hedgerows. The problem with crocosmia is that it is a wanderer and, because of this habit, a real garden bully, although I also think that there is something very cheery about it when it absorbs the particular grey Devon light we get over the Axe Vale, so I can be persuaded. On the other hand, I just know it will create a problem if I am not vigilant.

I also imported bindweed for the same reason and we have been trying to cope with that ever since. Our technique is to unwind it from whatever it is climbing up, transfer it to a bamboo cane to mark it, and then put it in a jam jar of commercial weed killer for a few weeks. We have found that to be quite effective. But bindweed is so invasive. It creeps up on you surreptitiously and it will go round anything from a telegraph pole to a Michaelmas daisy.

Last but not least, our very own enemy 'number one' is the buttercup. They certainly were here originally, together with the rabbits that must have frolicked with delight to see us providing them with not just mounds but superior drainage. You could say I inadvertently provided our Devon population of rabbits with the rabbit equivalent of highly desirable residences of Grand Design elegance and proportions, and with no planning permission required – rabbit heaven!

RIGHT Sedums and asters, *Aster amellus* 'King George' highlighted amongst the grasses

I was determined to make this section of the garden as labour saving as possible so, after planting, we covered the whole area with wood chips. We have a ready supply of these. I realised that if I were to pave or grass the central path, the birds, not to mention the rabbits, would be constantly scratching the chippings down onto it so I decided to wood chip the whole area, including the path, and that has worked really well.

The Grasses Garden of course benefited from the fifty years of experience I had built up from developing the other parts of the garden. Over this time I have come a long way from the young gardener who said 'It looks as though I'll be doing the garden then' when asked by a neighbour whose job that would be. One thing I have learnt is to be more disciplined in my gardening. The Grasses Garden in some sense marks my growing up as a gardener. For example I now know which danger weeds I will need to deal with and try to spray them off in the first few years after planting when there is still space

BELOW The view across the Grasses Garden from the seat with pampas grass, *Cortaderia selloana* in the background

RIGHT *Verbena bonariensis* underplanted with *Echium vulgare* 'Blue Bedder': Sally Newcomb

between the maturing specimens. From the quarry and through the years to the Grasses Garden I learnt that no gardener, whether working with a big or a small site, can set themselves against the conditions of the land being worked. Whatever the size of your garden, there are parts of it that have their own special micro-climates and frost pockets because frost is a fluid medium like water – here at Burrow Farm Gardens it flows down the slopes. I have needed to learn these subtle changes and work with them. The quarry was shady with some dry shade and a lot of wet shade and the Grasses Garden is my only well drained site right out in sun.

I am very appreciative of the privileges I have as a gardener and of the liberation of having the luxury of becoming more and more familiar with a different group of plants that will thrive in such contrasting areas, each with their own peculiarities, 'wants and needs'. I have never fallen out of love with a group of plants but I thrive on acquiring and finding out about new ones. When visiting

a nursery with my sister-in-law, Margaret, I can remember saying to her that I would buy the plant she was buying as well because, although it was not my present passion, it probably could be my next one. I cannot remember now what the plant was but I know I did not particularly like it at the time. For me, this is the thrill of gardening. There is a constant natural movement that comes with it. Nothing stays the same and you can never 'rest on your laurels'. Maybe through other gardens, chance conversations or the creativity of others you see how somebody has used something in a way you would never have thought of and the plant that you did not particularly value at one point in the life of your garden becomes a star of the future.

Something that is a continuous thread that runs throughout the whole of Burrow Farm Gardens and knits it together also became my main goal for the Grasses Garden. For me, it is necessary to try and achieve balance from all viewing perspectives. I would stand individual grass plants out there on a day

ABOVE *Verbena bonariensis*
and *Dierama igneum*
among the grasses: Sally
Newcomb

when it was not too windy and then plant them, when satisfied. I put all the asters and other plants as groups in drifts but, because they get so big, the only way to describe what I've done with them is 'spotting them around as sort of focal dots', although that is not an entirely satisfactory description. These 'focal dots' were planted first, then after that I threaded the asters in-between in drifts to keep that sinuous line which was so crucial.

With the Grasses Garden I did write things down because I did not feel I knew any of the plants well enough, like the asters and grasses and all their names, so I recorded them all on paper. Over the years I had learnt to do this with other, smaller, individual areas in the garden, drawing out the rough shape of the new border then putting in the main plants. My focal point for these designs would perhaps be one existing shrub or a tree on a promontory. Then having identified this 'marker' I would make lists of plants that I thought would associate well with that particular main plant and ones that would also suit the prevailing soil and weather conditions of the particular place. As you do this exercise you end up with groups of plants in different positions. The next step then becomes the easy one of in-filling between these imaginary clumps. I make extensive lists of plants that I feel will associate well together and pick the plants out of these lists. In the Grasses Garden my main palette was the asters and things like the sedums, persicarias, salvias, *Perovskia* 'Blue Spire' and origanums, all on the pinkish or blue spectrum and even the grasses I chose were ones with 'pinky' or 'mauvy' flowers. *Miscanthus nepalensis*, for example, is not in this garden because I felt that it would not have been the right shade for it, but I have got it elsewhere.

We are at the stage now where we have to keep chopping some of the bigger *Miscanthus nepalensis* in half then divide them up and pot them on to sell. Visitors do rave about it and even if they have never really liked grasses

before their visit, they become converts. The Grasses Garden is so far away from the popular view of pampas grass in the middle of the lawn. Here I have used pampas grass as an equivalent of a shrub or small tree, to be viewed through the intense autumn colour of the *Liquidambar styraciflua* and acers because then you get the totally different shape and colour of the whitish pampas flower and the contrast. That is how I like pampas grass to be used.

As far as maintenance is concerned, in the autumn or winter, depending on the weather, we go over the clumps of grasses like the *Miscanthus nepalensis* with the hedge trimmer. Our method is quite simple. We just hold the grass and cut through at the bottom. It is very easy. I also try and cut the ones that are going to self-seed before the winter. The evergreen grasses like *Stipa gigantea* need to be treated differently. We just comb out the dead leaves and cut the heads off so the Grasses Garden is low maintenance compared to some of the other areas in the garden.

The Grasses Garden fits in with the naturalistic look of the rest of the gardens and with the incorporation of the informal, naturally softened beauty that comes through the shape of the Vale and its ambient light. To enhance this look, as I created the gardens I purposefully tried to develop them so that they became increasingly wilder in a series of soft waves as the land slopes from the house down towards the Valley. As the garden has expanded this has happened quite naturally, although I am not sure I have succeeded in achieving it everywhere.

The Grasses Garden is not only a fitting celebration of our fifty years but perfectly reflects this philosophy and of course it has the added bonus of being at its best at the end of the summer. On reflection the Grasses Garden makes a fitting symbol to mark both an anniversary and the end of the summer garden season.

Chapter 8

From Bramble Patch to Azalea Glade and Weeds to a Wildflower Meadow

LEFT The wildflower meadow, shimmering with yellow buttercups, looking across to the valley and hills beyond

RIGHT The thatched summerhouse with *Cornus* 'Eddie's White Wonder' in the foreground

It was John Hawkins who helped me to build the thatched summerhouse that heralded the beginning of Azalea Glade. We began it in 2002, with our dog audience in tow. He and I did the stonework and the cobbled floor and then Kevin Tratt from down the road did the carpentry. I was keen that the finished build should not look like a bus shelter in the middle of a field, so I think perhaps I went a little bit over the top with 'chunkiness'. John Hawkins was not only good at building – he built not just this summerhouse, which was to be the first element of Azalea Glade, but also various other structures around the gardens – he was also adopted by a dog that is

memorable among my 'waifs and strays'. She loved him.

I have already mentioned that when John and I got married and came here to Burrow Farm various dogs appeared unannounced and completely out of the blue. One day, I saw an absolutely emaciated Greyhound on the road but I couldn't get anywhere near it so I came home and got some food but when I returned it was nowhere to be seen. I got in the car and drove round looking for the poor animal, including visiting a neighbouring farm. As Richard Lawrence, the farmer, and I were talking we suddenly saw it in one of his fields. We ventured out to try and get the dog

BELOW *Azalea amoenum*
in the foreground with
the large *Rhododendron
loderi* 'King George'
on the left and
Yakushimanum hybrids in
the centre

in the most extraordinary hailstorm I have ever experienced. It was a white blackout and the hailstones were huge and, of course, when it stopped the dog had disappeared again. In the end I went to the garage at the bottom of the road and asked them to look out for this greyhound. A little bit later on they saw it in their yard and eventually located it in one of their derelict cars. They looked after it and fed it for a few days but could not keep it because it fought with their greyhounds, so they asked me if I would have it, and of course I did.

She had apparently been running around the area for two years. Many people had seen her but nobody had been able to get near her. She was obviously quite a good 'rabbiter' because that was how she had been surviving. She was so thin and she had what looked like cigarette burns all over. We had to keep her on a lead for a while, but after a couple of months we felt confident that she would not

stray and took her along with the other dogs for a walk. Afterwards she came in and got into a chair and, as she was licking herself, I saw she had a huge gaping wound in her stomach where she had staked herself going through the hedge. I bundled her in the car and took her to the vet. I did not know whether to ask him to stitch her up, spay her while she was open or put her down. Anyway, they stitched her up. She was a lovely old thing. She had a terrible fear of men, except of course she got used to my John fairly quickly because he was around all the time but the first man she really took to other than John was John Hawkins. He used to come every day and have lunch in his car. He put a rug on the back seat for the greyhound and brought her treats. She thought he was the 'bees knees'. She used to garden with us like Tilly does now but she was very thin-skinned and felt the cold. She would not give up

ABOVE Azalea Glade
with a mix of deciduous
azaleas in shades of yellow
and orange

though. She would sit beside us with her teeth chattering but she would not go in until we had finished for the day.

Just beyond and up the hill from the summerhouse that we had by this time completed was a natural dell that was full of bracken and brambles and the home to numerous rabbits. The following winter, when John Hawkins and I had a little spare time, I decided to clear this vegetation and thin the trees from the dell in the hope that the rabbits would move further away. The benefit of winter tree work is there are no nesting birds to worry about. We cut down a large conifer but after we had nearly finished clearing it all up I noticed a young bird peering up at me from a heap of sawdust. I was to learn, at a later date, that pigeons breed all through the year. It appeared we had felled the tree along with pigeon's nest and chick. My dilemma was what to do with it. My helpers made

several unsavoury suggestions that I certainly was not going to follow. I rang Secret World in Somerset who were very helpful and said if I was to take it to them they would be open for the next hour. I set off immediately and just made it before they closed. They inspected the chick and thought it would be capable of surviving. I was pleased that my mission had been successful, though mindful of petrol costs for rescuing one baby pigeon. Imagine my horror when a few days later I received a sixty-pound speeding fine as well as another three points on my driving licence. Sometimes life just doesn't seem fair. My only hope was that it didn't end up as pigeon pie on somebody's plate. Azalea Glade began to take shape from this point.

When we started the clearing I realised very quickly that the soil was the best anywhere in the garden – a friable greensand. Of course this was irresistible, and in no time

ABOVE AND RIGHT
Cypripedium hybrids
given to me by the Dutch
Royal Horticultural
Society on their recent
visit to the garden

at all I had planted it up with quite a few deciduous Azaleas, candelabra primulas, ferns, trilliums, with erythroniums, cyclamen and cypripedium hybrids. Snowdrops, bluebells and primroses spread amongst them giving earlier colour.

Here in Azalea Glade we have a spring that runs down to provide the water for the ponds located at the bottom of the garden. But even with all this change, the rabbits are still there!

I have places in the gardens that are favourite spots at different times over the year because the views, light and atmosphere change with the seasons. In spring, for me, it is the Woodland Garden before the leaves come out so you can actually look down into it and see the contours of the ground that are quite extraordinary. That gives me a huge

amount of pleasure. I would deny being a snowdrop enthusiast at any other time of the year but ask me in February and I would have to admit there is something special about snowdrops. They are the real signs of the beginning of spring for me because their pristine whiteness makes such a contrast to the little rotting heaps of wind-blown autumn leaves caught up in the foliage of other plants. There are minute differences between the species but, for me, the ones I like the best are the larger flowered ones with substantial petals that do not open out too widely, like *Galanthus* 'Straffan' and the various *elwesii* snowdrops.

It was in the spring of the year 2000, as I was appreciating these particular joys, when Tony said 'I've got a digger on hire and we have got half an hour to spare Mum, so is there is anything you want done?' Having said that the Millennium Garden, which we had just finished, was going to be my last bit of new garden, I confess that I had already been looking at the bit of boggy field down at the bottom thinking 'I wonder whether a pond down there would hold water or not'.

ABOVE In Azalea Glade looking towards the wildlife ponds across the deciduous azaleas with *Philadelphus coronarius* 'Aureus' in the foreground on the right

RIGHT *Trillium chloropetalum* growing in the moist shade

I asked Tony if the digger could go down there and dig just a test hole, sort of four foot by four foot and four foot deep. My idea was that we could then leave it for the whole summer and see whether it would hold water. The digger trundled down there and started digging. I have a slide that I use in my various talks of Tony enveloped in this huge excavation because he definitely got a bit carried away. In the course of doing his 'half hour' excavation the digger went through a field drain that was running quite well. At this point it became obvious that we had gone too far to go back and we discovered that it was very good clay which would make a lovely pond. We decided we might as well go for it so it wasn't half an hour later but more like a week later that we stopped digging.

We put topsoil all round the top of the excavation and that was when I realised that it was going to look like a muddy mess for the whole of the summer because that spring it just poured with rain. The day he finished it water just rushed down the hillside and the next morning when I was going to go and 'puddle the clay' and pick out the stones and make it as watertight as I could, we already could not get in it. It was over the top of our wellingtons so we had to leave it as it was. We had a real panic all day because we realised that we had not thought about where the overflow was going to be and that the whole of the bottom side was actually a dam because the ground slopes down. We frantically dug an overflow so it did not totally collapse and before we knew what had happened the water was up at the top. I shrugged my shoulders philosophically and thought 'well, I will have to just leave it as a pond out in the middle of the field' because at that time

ABOVE The pond later in the first year with the wild ducks that flew in

it was outside the garden. But of course, typically for me, I got a bit carried away with my muddy excavation. Ideas for improvement were running round my head. I had some *Gunnera manicata* that I wanted to plant and some grasses and this and that, so I did some planting up at one end and against the fence right next to the pond, then I thought 'this is a bit silly, I think I can do a bit better than this'. Nearby, was a splendid oak tree. One evening when we had finished work I was telling my husband about a bench we had been making under this big 500 year-old oak tree. My thinking was that if it became part of this, to date rather hesitant, planting it would 'make' the space by providing focal interest while at the same time solving my dilemma about improving the existing planting. In reply my husband just said 'You can't move a 500 year-old oak tree into the garden'. My immediate response was 'You could if you moved the fence to the other side of it!' So we did. We moved the fence round the other side of the oak tree and in this way another part of the gardens came into being. From having put the bench there with a little bit of planting to admire, the area just kept growing like 'Topsy'. Thinking about it, I would say that is how most of Burrow Farm Gardens developed. I always think the saying 'Mighty oaks from little acorns grow' is very apt for Burrow Farm Gardens, in more ways than one.

One of the most rewarding things about doing the pond was the day the wild ducks flew in because I felt that was nature accepting what we had made. It's rather like planting a tree and then you spot a bird sitting in it. It's just as rewarding. The planting continued round there with quite

ABOVE The two ducks
on the pond with their
floating residence made
by my husband John in
the background under the
large *Gunnera manicata*
leaves. The tree on the
left is the swamp cypress,
Taxodium distichum that
colours up beautifully in
the autumn

a few deciduous azaleas and some magnolias and *Metasequoia glyptostrobides* 'Gold Rush'. Initially, one *Gunnera manicata* was planted at each end, bringing more of the garden to life. The wild ducks still come and go each night and if you sit down there late in the evening you can often spot them flying in and landing with a splash for their evening sojourn.

I was not going to introduce any other ducks to this pond but Lynne, one of the lady gardeners, said they were about to cull the ducks at the place where her husband worked. She asked me if I would 'home' any. I said no because I felt I could not spare the time to go and shut them up every night. Then we discussed the idea of a floating duck shelter that would mean I didn't have to shut them up. My next excuse was that I thought there was every possibility the foxes would still get them but Lynne pointed out that if

any of these condemned ducks had one day on my pond it would be one day longer than they would have where they were. Lynne has grown to know me very well over the years and she knew very well that I would not be able to turn down a 'rescue'. I was easily persuaded and had two of these Aylesbury ducks.

We put them down in our pond. Of course there was nothing to stop them leaving but they appeared delighted with their new home. We went to have coffee and then went down to check on them but they had gone. We could see one in the distance but could not see the other one anywhere. We managed to shepherd the one back and went round the lanes in the car, eventually finding the other one in a holly hedge in the neighbour's garden. It had got a long way considering it could not fly. Luckily the neighbour had a type of giant fishing net, used to catch poultry, but trying to catch that duck in a hedge was not easy. It took four of us about an hour but eventually we caught it and took it back to the pond. I put some electrified pig netting round the pond and both ducks stayed there happily for some time. During the summer we had to take the fence away but by that time they had both lasted well over the extra day Lynne had given them, and in fact they lived here very happily for two years, enjoyed by visitors and gardeners alike.

Eventually, and almost inevitably, a fox got one of them, leaving the other companion-less. It was just at the time of bird flu when you had to shut poultry indoors so we housed it up in the stables. This all happened just before Christmas. I also enquired in various places whether there was another Aylesbury duck I could buy but they were all 'oven ready' by that time so none were available for companion duties! Somebody told me they knew someone who had some large silver Appleyard ducks so I went miles to Crediton, got one of them and put it in the stable. The staff here had a bit of a sad Christmas

BELOW Deciduous azaleas looking towards the wildflower meadow area

RIGHT Modern inventions can make gardening easier. Showing my sister-in-law around the Wildflower Meadow: Sally Newcomb

thinking of the solitary survivor, little knowing that our original was now happily ensconced with a mate.

When we got the all clear we put them both back in the pond. The single sole surviving duck eventually fell prey to a fox too so we were just left with the one silver Appleyard. I could not make up my mind whether to wait for the fox to get that one too or go and get it a mate, because I knew if I did the chances were the fox would come and get that survivor too! But at the time of writing, I've weakened and we've now got her a rather magnificent partner. They seem to be getting along well, fingers crossed. Maybe there'll be the patter of tiny webbed feet?

For a time our ducks swam their territory with the rescue fish that somebody brought to us in two dustbins and, of course, the ever-present moorhens. It was lovely to see the fish

swimming around until the heron discovered them. So we had to make a scarecrow out of whatever we had lying around. It was not the most handsome of figures with its bucket for a head, all in all a very Heath Robinson affair, better at causing hilarity among visitors to the gardens than actually seeing off the heron. All I can say is, we did try. Artistic gardeners we may be but sculptors we are so obviously not! The scarecrow is no longer there but on a more positive and ethereal note our pond has attracted much more desirable wildlife in the form of masses of butterflies, damselflies and dragonflies. These are much more entertaining than our scarecrow and are a joy to watch for as long as you have got the time to 'just sit' and be still, something I must confess I have never been very good at.

We created the Wildflower Meadow in a field we have always called 'rag', where we

RIGHT *Papaver somniferum* (opium poppy) with seed heads contrasting with the golden grass in the Wildflower Meadow: Sally Newcomb

LEFT P*apaver somniferum* (opium poppy) self seeding among the azaleas: Sally Newcomb

ABOVE White robin *Lychnis flos-cuculi*, with visiting butterfly

grazed the cows or horses. Over the years this bit of land came to be populated by docks and creeping thistle and other plants like patches of stinging nettles and rushes. Obviously, before you start introducing any other flowers you have got to get rid of those so it was a question of spot spraying for about four years to eradicate these 'nasties'. Meanwhile we just cut the whole site for hay.

One year we had a particularly wet spring and consequently were not able to mow the lawn in the garden for several weeks. To our astonishment we started to find quite a few common spotted orchids growing in the lawns. Michael, my grandson, who is especially fond of orchids, decided that he would dig them up one by one and transplant them to the spot we had designated for the Wildflower Meadow. What we did not realise was that there were so many of them. He did over two hundred in the first year and then there were another hundred the following year and they not only survived but are now thriving. At the same time we introduced 'Yellow Rattle', *Rhinanthus minor*, which is parasitic on grasses, reducing their vigour and allowing the wildflowers to compete. Each year we have gradually spread the Yellow Rattle over the whole area so it is now quite manageable grass. We have to dig up the odd patch of rushes that still appears and have tried desperately to introduce oxeye daisies,

Leucanthemum vulgare, but with very little success, possibly because it is a little on the damp side. Infuriatingly these are one of those plants that tend to flourish on roadside verges and poor soil where there is not much competition from other plants, but I am still hopeful. I have a patch of white silver birch, *Betula utilis* var. *jacquemontii* with the white stems I planted down there and I dream of establishing a mass of white oxeye daisies inside their circle of trunks. I know it would be spectacular. So far I have got one! On the other hand, these daisies flourish in the rock garden on the other side of the gardens where we have introduced more gravel. You could even say they are invasive – you just cannot keep them out of there, proving that plants choose their own places and are not always obedient to 'garden interventions' or the dreams of gardeners.

In the meadow there are also masses of buttercups and the 'bacon and egg plant', *Lotus corniculatus*, Bird's-foot trefoil, and blue Veronica. All these plants are spread over the whole meadow and then, around the edge near the hedge, there are a lot of bluebells, foxgloves and primroses as well as wood anemones. The whole area is two or three acres, with plans to introduce more plants like fritillaries. There is a particularly suitable area for these between the standing stones and the ditch and I have been introducing them there, partly as seed and partly as bulbs. Unfortunately rabbits really love the fritillary flowers but I am hoping that, when there are enough, this plundering by the rabbits will not be quite so obvious. My theory, and I am sticking to it, is that there are fields of fritillaries and I suppose when you get up to a certain number they cannot eat them all. I am concentrating the fritillaries in the damp area because the grass has to be mown at different times. We do encourage some wild life in Burrow Farm Gardens because that 'fits' with our naturalistic philosophy, but I have to admit we get a bit fed up with constantly

LEFT Common spotted orchid hybrids in profusion with Lady's Smock, *Cardamine pratensis* and Marsh Bedstraw, *Galium palustre*

BELOW Betony, *Stachys officinalis*, growing in the wildflower area

battling with others. We want the dragonflies, butterflies and a multitude of other insects but the marauding rabbits and deer can stay away because they can destroy an area in a night. They are here regularly and their destructive antics can be heart breaking! In 2017, we were really caught by the fact that by the time the orchid seed was ready and we could cut the field, the weather had turned and we just had to cut it and dump the hay because it was too wet. It made quite a mess

as well. I have never known a year like it and hopefully it will not be repeated.

We started the wild flower area about three or four years ago but the spraying, as I have said, was done over a number of years beforehand so it has been a labour of love. I have decided never to introduce any plants that would occur in a cornfield mix into this area. I only use those plants that would develop naturally in these conditions and those that are encouraged by the management of the area and the fact that the grasses are not so vigorous here. Perhaps there are only a few species but that is fine. Camassias are popular for example and I have them in long grass between the shrubs in other parts of the garden but I would not want them in the Wildflower Meadow. We also have quite a lot of wild daffodils down near the edges of the trees where it is damper. We have a big drift of them at the top of the area as well because, years and years ago, our neighbour came down and dug some of these wild daffodils out of a field of ours and planted them in her garden. They then seeded back through the hedge – a happy accident of nature.

Because there was a very wet patch in this field we decided to drain it by digging two wildlife ponds to collect the water together and then pipe it to the existing ditch. This has worked extremely well and the lower part of the field has dried up considerably and has controlled the rushes that were beginning to get established.

The Wildflower Meadow and ponds have been a welcome addition to Burrow Farm Gardens. If I was to use the analogy of a particularly fine Old Master painting I would say they have provided or are able to give, those subtle tints and hues that have brought a depth to the gardens as a whole. The most exciting prospect is that the Wildflower Meadow particularly is a painting in progress, with all the unpredictability and promise that implies.

Chapter 9

Developments:
Looking Beyond the Closed Gate

LEFT The lovely old gate Geranium x magnificum mingling happily to the front and *Rosa Bonica* peeping through the other side of it: Mark Bolton

BELOW Snow in Devon: looking down towards the valley through snow covered trees

So often the development of a new area is set in motion by a chance happening. In Autumn 2017 a tree nursery nearby was selling up. Tony, Penny, Sue and I went to the auction where they were selling twenty thousand trees. Some were container grown, the rest were field grown and these had to be dug up and removed from the site within the next two weeks. The sale was hectic and there were large numbers of bidders so it was quite difficult to see what you were bidding for, hence I ended up with several surprises – for instance five white Mulberries. The purchase of several different cultivars of prunus, among other trees, has led to the development of a

small plantation at the top of the Wildflower Meadow. I was particularly pleased with the purchase of a fine weeping Beech tree, *Fagus sylvatica*, and a weeping Hornbeam, *Carpinus betulus* 'Pendula'. I have planted a group of *Cornus capitata*, some snakebark maples and a *Betula* 'Fetisowii' that will have peeling chalk white bark in time. I hope this mix will be attractive all year with the Wildflower Meadow all around them and mown paths threading through to the seats at the viewpoint. Two seats at the viewpoint are dedicated to John and Peggy Perryman, my very first garden volunteers.

Just lately, as well as clearing and re-cutting

ABOVE *Camassia leichtlinii* subsp. *suksdorfii* Caerulea Group naturalised beside an old stone trough

RIGHT Summerhouse with *Acer palmatum* framing and foregrounding

FOLLOWING PAGES Aerial picture taken in June 2018 showing the full thirteen acres of garden in its setting

out the stream that runs through the glade in the Woodland Garden and installing some very grand gates up near the Rose and Millennium Gardens to act as a deterrent to deer, we have also been cutting down the holly trees on the far perimeter of the Wildflower Meadow in order to thicken up the base to form a good holly hedge. This has been energetic, warm work with bonfires to be tended in some of the coldest weather I can remember. So much of gardening is about doing the jobs that are best suited to the weather and soil conditions.

Over the years, as the garden has developed the business has grown with it. Plant fairs, open-air theatre and weddings are a regular yearly occurrence and John Horsey has been running a number of weekly gardening courses using our lecture room as a base. His students appreciate a walk through the garden when they are here throughout the year so we have now constructed hard paths throughout the garden to make it accessible whatever the conditions underfoot. This involved raking out and spreading twenty-four tonnes of hardcore that I discovered to my cost is something that should not be done in your late seventies.

This book has been my story of the trials and tribulations of creating Burrow Farm Gardens. It features my family, dogs and other helpers who have become part of the extended family over the years but overall it is about the hugely rewarding experience of creating a garden from scratch out of a piece of Devon farmland. I have tried to present the garden as a series of images through the unveiling of different views that reflect the vista of the Axminster valley as it plays across the eye from different parts of the garden. I hope this book will encourage you to visit the garden and that the garden will give you as much pleasure as it has given me over the years.

The End... for now

Index

Garden Notes

Garden Notes

Garden Notes

Burrow Farm Gardens
East Devon's Secret Garden

ICON KEY

⭐ *You are here*

👫♿ Toilets / Disabled facilities

🍴☕ Tea Room

🌸 Nursery

🛍 Gift Shop

🐚 Viewpoint

KEY

A   Courtyard Garden

B   Terrace Garden

C   Rock Garden

D   Grasses Garden

E   Millennium Garden

F   Rose Garden

G   Ha-ha View

H   Woodland Pond

I   Lake

J   Wildflower Meadow

K   Wildlife Ponds

L   Azalea Glade

M   Summerhouse

N   Japanese Azalea Lawn

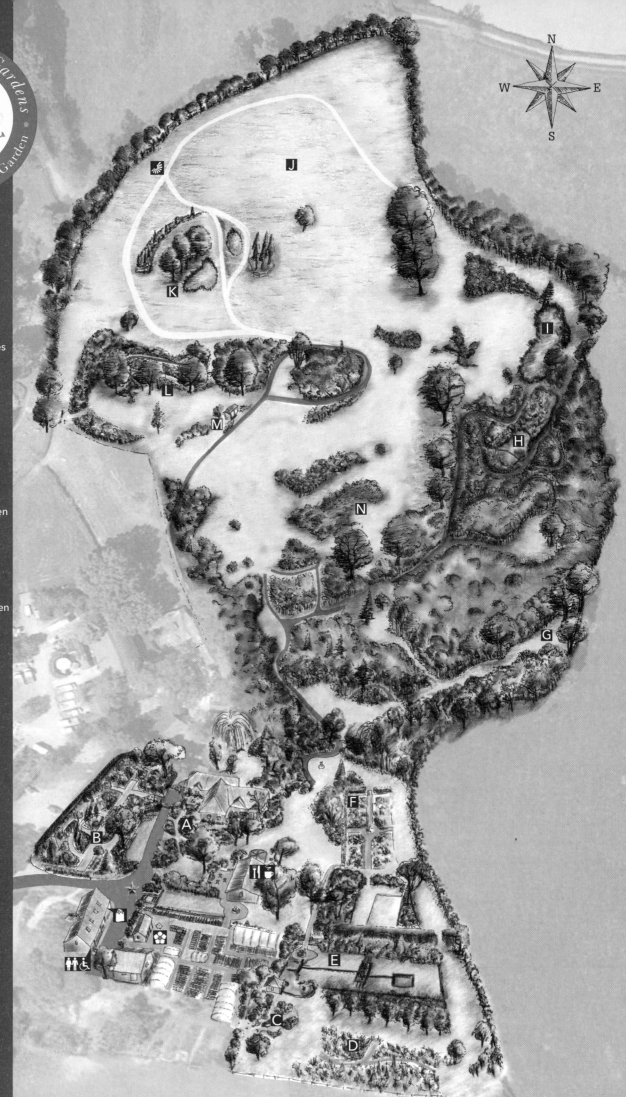

Welcome to
Burrow Farm Gardens

We moved to Burrow Farm in 1959 and John built up a dairy herd while I started making a garden firstly as a hobby, then with the intention of opening it to the public.

There was no garden here at all when we arrived and I started by making a small garden around the house (in between having four children), but then extended it to the old Roman clay pit which was full of brambles, nettles and fallen trees.

In the first few years I concentrated on clearing the scrub and planting some of the main new trees and shrubs. We lived in a timber and asbestos bungalow, that was here when we came, until 1993 when we built the present house on the same site.

The courtyard and terrace garden were started the same year. The Rose Garden built in 1985 was the first area to be constructed with a formal design, but the planting has always been very informal with old roses, geraniums and other herbaceous plants.

The Millennium Garden was one of the most ambitious projects undertaken and took nearly two years to complete. The lake was dug the same year and was followed shortly by the planting of cornus, azaleas, etc in that area.

We built the thatched summerhouse in 2002, also the hard track out to that area to enable work to be carried out throughout the year. The planting was done mainly during the following two winters. The craft shop and lecture room were built in 2006.

The soil is a neutral clay, but with the annual leaf-fall from the oak trees it is suitable for the growing of rhododendrons and azaleas.

In recent years my grandson Michael has taken a major role in the development of the garden and the business as a whole. The garden has always involved the whole family in various ways either working part time in the garden or tearoom.

We have various part time workers and volunteers in the garden and all are able to bring their different skills to the various projects and day to day maintenance.

What started out as a hobby has become my lifetimes work. The gardens now cover over 13 acres. We do own 35 acres, so who knows!

I hope you enjoy the garden as much as I do.

Mary Benger

Rose Garden

Wild Flower Meadow

Terrace Garden

Lake

The Grasses Garden